LONDON TRANSPORT

BUSES & COACHES

1955

LONDON TRANSPORT
BUSES & COACHES

1955

John A.S. Hambley

Published in 1995 by
IMAGES

in conjunction with
JOHN A. S. HAMBLEY
7 Linden Road,
Dunstable,
Beds. LU5 4NZ

Additional text and research by David A. Ruddom

British Library Cataloguing in Publication Data
A catalogue record for this book is available from the British Library

ISBN 1 897817 66 5

Front cover photograph:
RF2 could not get any closer to the main entrance to St.Paul's Cathedral if it tried as it stands in St.Paul's Churchyard. Now finished in all over green paintwork, which it gained on its recent overhaul, the bus operates from Camberwell garage on a Seeing London, City Tour. Although this vehicle moved around to various garages in its early life it always returned to this South London home as if the staff could not bear to part with it. The different styles in the ornamental bollards at the steps of the Cathedral are a result of earlier enemy action where several had to be replaced after a nearby bomb wrecked them. The tourist activity at this Cathedral was obviously less frenetic than it is today. (Lens of Sutton)

Back cover photograph:
Looking quite immaculate, GF7254 belies the age of its chassis which once operated with London Transport as LT1000 carrying a double deck body illustrated in the 1954 book of this series. The coach keeps another full fronted example company while they are parked in Francis Street just off Vauxhall Bridge Road. Since this was one of the vehicles with the special LGOC "CC" type experimental chassis one wonders how the subsequent owners managed to keep such a unique vehicle on the road for such a length of time. (D.A.Jones)

Designed and produced by Images (Publishing) Malvern Ltd.
Printed and bound by Hillman Printers (Frome) Ltd.

There won't be many empty seats once GS33 has taken on board the rest of the intending passengers at Onslow Street Bus Station in Guildford on this sunny Saturday 2nd July. It looks as though some of them at least are heading for a picnic at a beauty spot like Newlands Corner. Over in the next bay stands a vehicle of the Aldershot and District Traction Company Ltd. (J.H.Aston)

Acknowledgements

I should like to give my cordial thanks to everyone who has contributed to this book with photographs, information or any other material.

I must also express my gratitude towards the London Transport enthusiasts and historians all around the world who now correspond on a variety of topics relating to the buses and coaches that have been operated in the capital principally by London Transport.

Much greatly appreciated help and patience has been shown to me by David Ruddom, so much so that without his tireless efforts these books would be that much the poorer in the printed word. A further special thank you is extended to the photographers and enthusiasts whose collections of photographs have been used and without whose help this book would never have come to fruition. They are: Norman Anscombe, J.H.Aston, C.Carter, Frank Church, Alan B.Cross, John Fozard, John Gascoine, J.C.Gillham, Peter Gomm, P.Gulland, W.J.Haynes, Roy Hobbs, F.W.Ivey, David Jones, Don.A.Jones, A.J.Kingett, W.R.Legg, John Lines, The London Trolleybus Preservation Society, L.E.Mallett, P.J.Malsher, Roy Marshall, Gerald Mead, W.Montgomery, The National Tramway Museum, A.G.Newman, J.G.E.Nye, The Omnibus Society, A.D.Packer, John Pilgrim, J.H.Price, Norman Rayfield, Geoff Rixon, David A.Ruddom, Michael Rooum, N. Rothon, D.Trevor Rowe, Lyndon Rowe, R.H.G.Simpson, John Smith of Lens of Sutton, John G.S.Smith, B. Speller, Sheila Taylor and the staff of the London Transport Museum, R.Wellings and A.M.Wright. Last but not least to my wife Iris and David's wife Enid a whole hearted thank you for having kept David and myself fed and watered through many sessions of deliberations.

Publisher's Note

Somewhere in the region of two hundred photographers or owners of collections of photographs have now offered help with this ever expanding series of books. Many exciting prints are held on file or known to be in enthusiast's collections and which will eventually be used.

If you ever photographed a London bus or coach, be it a single print or colour slide or a larger number, then please do get in touch with the author whose address appears on the reverse of the title page.

The author tries very hard to acknowledge all letters received and is grateful for all the constructive comments made. Please be patient if you do not receive an answer as soon as you would have liked.

A listing of all identifiable London vehicles shown in the books so far published is now available but only direct from the author in Dunstable. It may be had in either route number or fleet number order at a cost of £4.50 each inclusive of post and packing.

Introduction

In 1955 the pinnacle with regard to the number of buses and coaches operated by London Transport had now passed and a steady decline in the number of vehicles owned will be witnessed in the following years. A great number of buses and coaches had been scrapped or disposed of since the cessation of hostilities in 1945 with a slightly higher number of replacements being put into service. Somewhere in the region of 8,000 new diesel powered vehicles together with a small number of trolleybuses had been purchased, set against a figure of a few hundred less diesel and petrol engined vehicles plus a small number of trolleybuses having been disposed of. However, the trams had been completely eradicated from the streets of the capital with the overall result that fewer vehicles were actually on the road.

Several reasons have been mentioned in earlier volumes as to the reasons for this fall off but car ownership must be singled out as being the major factor possibly added to a steady decline in the population figures for Inner London. This together with staff recruitment problems and dissatisfaction with service provision had resulted in the Ministry of Transport setting up a Committee of Inquiry under the chairmanship of Mr.S.P.Chambers which produced its lengthy report in February 1955. There were ninety two paragraphs of "Conclusions and Recommendations" and looking back from our vantage point some forty years later it is interesting to see how some of these were implemented in later years and others totally ignored.

One of the earliest recommendations to be ignored was that rejecting the idea of limited stop services; London Transport introducing just such things during the year on routes 52A, 130, 174 and 212. Another conclusion was that independent operators should be allowed to start services which London Transport were unable to implement and before the year was out West London Coachways had started their Feltham to Bedfont service which remained in the private sector for many years. Other ideas such as special services in Central London using "standee" buses took longer to come to fruition but there is no doubt that the Chambers Report had its effects on the transport scene in London.

During the year further non-standard classes of vehicle were withdrawn and by the end of 1955 the aim of standardisation had almost totally been achieved. All that remained outside the RT/RTL/RTW/RLH/RF/GS classes were the 131 strong TD class and about 100 T class single deckers although not all of these latter vehicles were in passenger service. Even within the RT class all of the 2RT2 variety were withdrawn from passenger service with the exception of seven which were repainted into Country Area livery and retained for the operation of Route 327 which traversed a weak bridge at Broxbourne.

Only one new vehicle was delivered to the Executive in the twelve months of 1955, this being the second Routemaster, RM2, which joined RM1 in undertaking various tests to determine the eventual design of London Transport's next generation of standard vehicles. RM1 and RM2 were originally allocated the registration numbers OLD862 and OLD863, notably unfortunate lettering for the so-called "Bus of the Future". In December they were re-registered SLT56 and SLT57 although they never actually carried the original registrations.

A number of new vehicles delivered during the previous year were still in store and these were RT4727, 4729 – 4759, 4761 – 4792 and RTL1568 – 1600 and 1602 – 1631. It would transpire that these would eventually enter service gradually in 1956, 1958 and 1959.

127 vehicles were withdrawn from service in 1955 and this figure was made up of the final 20 STLs dating from 1945/46; the remainder of the STD class which totalled 63; the unique G436 – a Guy Arab chassis equipped with a Guy body to Park Royal design; a further 24 T class single deckers and finally 19 of the so-called "pre-war" RTs.

Most of the withdrawn vehicles were sold for further service, several being exported in particular to Yugoslavia as some pictures in this volume show. A small number were scrapped or, as in the case of RT106, converted into service vehicles. 27 of the STD class remained in store until being sold for further service abroad in the following year.

One overseas trip was made by a London Transport owned double decker during the year and on this occasion RTL1117, overhauled the previous month, made the sea voyage to Holland leaving England on 16th May. It arrived back on 8th August, having spent some time involved with the Arnhem week celebrations among other duties, and resumed normal work on 5th September from West Green garage.

In the first half of the year a great upheaval of buses took place whereby it was aimed to standardise the fleet in each engineering district on either AEC or Leyland vehicles. South west London became Leyland and South east London AEC which was rather the reverse of previous practice.

One very noticeable change that began in 1955 was a redesign of the blind layouts, particularly on the RT family. Full blind displays had been introduced in 1950 and initially the route blinds had five lines encompassing as much information as could be fitted in using a mixture of place names and street names. Later the five line display was modified to use only one place name per line but in the year under review a new four line display was introduced which spread fairly rapidly throughout the system. In addition a thicker style of numbers appeared on certain single deck blinds and examples of these changes can be found in the pages of this volume.

On the service and route side of operations 1955 was the most dramatic since the end of the War. For the first time draconian schedule cuts were introduced and proceeded with. While there were service introductions – for example Heathrow Central received its first regular daily bus services during the year – and the usual enhanced summer services, including a large excursion programme dominated by London Airport day trips, these were overshadowed by the severity of the cuts. Whereas in the first five years of the nineteen fifties scheduled mileage had only been reduced by 0.3%, in 1955 alone the reduction was 5%. Each schedule reduction produced a staff reaction, sometimes merely local, sometimes system wide but the pattern was set and this reaction culminated in the disastrous strike of 1958 which resulted in even more cuts but that remains to be told in surveys of future years.

RT371 was a long stay resident at Upton Park garage and during its period at this East End base it received two overhauls, and not until its third such venture did the bus move on to Leyton garage. The date is 21st May and the bus waits at Cyprus – in east London rather than the eastern Mediterranean – ready for another journey on route 101 to Wanstead Station. This was the first post-war year in which the route did not receive its customary summer weekend extension beyond Wanstead to Lambourne End. (J.H.Aston)

Croxley Metropolitan Line Station provides the resting place for RT4164 which is working a cross-Watford short on route 321 which at its fullest worked between Uxbridge and Luton. This bus correctly carries a short working route blind which probably indicates a conscientious conductor. (J.Gascoine collection)

T794 takes further passengers on board for its journey to Rainham via the uninspiring roads of route 371 from this bus stop in London Road, Grays. RT4042 stands at the stop further along the road. (R.Wellings)

A fine study of the market place at Skopje, a predominantly Moslem area juding by the two minarets towering in the distance. An unidentified STL registered M411, of which the M indicates it is registered in the Republic of Macedonia, then part of Yugoslavia, is parked someway from the crowded footpath and bus stop. The flag for this is attached to a telegraph pole and suggests it is served by routes 9, 8 and 3. The bus is working the latter route in this picture taken on 2nd September. (J.C.Gillham)

With the Rainham Church peering through the lush greenery, RT4194 rests before a journey on Route 328C to Aveley Estate, Elan Road. This bus had been garaged at Grays since the introduction of RT operation on the former Eastern National routes in that area in the latter months of 1951. (R.Wellings)

Standing in the yard at Catford garage in September, RT1518 carries a blind display for route 89, the via blind of which is in the experimental three line style which was not perpetuated. This RT arrived at this south east London garage in the last month of 1953 from its previous home at Forest Gate. More stable compatriots including RT588, RT2129 and RT2408 keep it company. (Peter Gulland)

RT4172, garaged at Garston, operates duty GR49 on the somewhat elusive route 301A to the Ovaltine Works at Kings Langley. The bus is seen at Watford Junction prior to commencing a journey on this works service for the convenience of employees at this well known establishment. (R.Wellings)

With a dry wintry background RF255, bound for Wrotham on route 703, appears to have generated no patronage at this rather uninviting slab of concrete. The driver is encased in his heavyweight top coat and the passengers are similarly dressed suggesting the meagre warmth of the coach interior is greatly valued by those within. (Peter Gomm collection)

STD140, complete with recently converted full blind display, heads for Debden Station on route 167 in its last winter in service on the streets of London as will be seen later in this volume. This particular route was a post-war development commencing in 1948 to serve the new housing being built in this part of Essex and north-east London. (J.G.S.Smith collection)

RTW38 stands alongside some wartime prefab type housing and a somewhat enigmatic road sign. Route 100, renumbered from 623 in October 1934, was the long standing replacement for the Barking trams which ran between that town and the huge Beckton gas works complex. This is a remarkable photo in that most buses operating this sporadic service worked off route 15 and the blind displays suffered accordingly. However on this occasion RTW38 not only has the correct full blind display but a "100" route plate has also been fitted on the offside. (D.A.Ruddom collection)

RTL and RTW class vehicles began to arrive at Putney Bridge garage in March as part of the first programme whereby different engineering districts within the Central Area would be either AEC or Leyland territories. RTL1065 works route 14 to Hornsey Rise on 20th March having been overhauled the previous month following its years since new at Clapham garage. (W.Legg)

Plumstead Common looking bleak and cold on 17th February plays host to RTL1556 as it waits to take up duties on a journey to Camden Town on route 53 as AM6. Two months later the bus was transferred to Chelverton Road, Putney garage as part of the Leyland for AEC bus transfers and RTs found a home at Plumstead garage. (W.Legg)

Ex STL2058 seen in Novi Sad, Serbia carries Yugoslavian registration number C5461 and is a 4/9STL15 with rebuilt platform area. It is now established this picture dates from 1954 but the scene in Serbia was felt to be worth leaving in this volume. (N.N.Forbes/National Tramway Museum)

This handsome view of TD16 taken on 24th September at Kingston Station shows to good effect the pleasing appearance of the early post-war type bodywork produced by Weymann at their Addlestone factory. Of standard provincial design, originally with seating for 33 passengers and fitted with sliding ventilators, they were of composite construction on a chassis with a 17'6" wheelbase. This bus was withdrawn from service in August 1957 and eventually exported to Ceylon as were twenty four of the thirty one vehicles which comprised the 1TD1 batch, all of which started their lives at Muswell Hill garage. (J.C.Gillham)

Premier Travel of Cambridge operated a number of STL type vehicles and ex-STL1746, now their number 91, stands at the Drummer Street Bus Station in Cambridge on 7th May. Later in the day the bus would move on to the stand to pick up for the service to Great Chishill, a village lying just east of Royston.

(J.C.Gillham)

The only summer RTL1356 was to operate from Clapham garage while it lacked trafficators was the one now being reviewed. Incredible how parking areas like this were so freely available, wouldn't it be a joy to find such a spot in today's driving conditions. (J.Gascoine collection)

Included in the last batch of the STD class to be withdrawn from service in February was STD163. Here, carrying a full set of route blinds for which it was originally designed in 1946 but never obtained until its last few months in service with LTE, it is seen at Victoria Station forecourt. Route 38A which operated between this terminus and Loughton Station was operated by Leyton and Loughton garages and the latter operated these Leyland Titan PD1 vehicles until post war RT types replaced them in February 1955. (A.J.Kingett)

A piece of history in the making could be the term given to this photograph of RT1420, the only Craven bodied RT not to be disposed of to Birds Commercial Motors of Stratford-upon-Avon. On 27th July, while in use as a Green Line relief from Windsor garage, it struck the low bridge in Coombe Road outside Norbiton Station sustaining irreparable body damage. How ironic that the front advertisements should read "Make Slough the Safety Town" – I suppose Norbiton didn't matter! Eventually the body, number 2699, was removed and scrapped. It was in June 1956 that the body from 1019J which had previously been fitted to RT19 and originally to RT1, number 18246, was mounted on to the six year old chassis to form service vehicle 1037J as a mobile instruction unit. Eventually regaining its RT1 fleet number and original registration, EYK396, the vehicle, after many vicissitudes, can still be seen from time to time at rallies and functions and is now preserved by Peter Gomm. (J.C.Gillham)

The date is 21st May and at Watford numerically the first of the Craven bodied RTs, RT1402, works on route 346 to Oxhey Estate. Those were the days when on a Friday night and for a stay of eight or fifteen days you could use the Starlight Special to Glasgow or Edinburgh for the princely sum of 70/- return (£3.50 in decimal currency). (G.Mead)

On 20th January changes were made to routes 396 and 396A in line with the continuing New Town expansion at Harlow. Red liveried RT1478, which normally resides at Leyton garage but here loaned to Epping, is seen in service on the extended route 396A. The destination blind for the new terminus at Hare Street is provided but the 396 number and a chalked route blind "396A POST OFFICE & HARE ST" has to suffice. The picture is taken on the new extension at the junction of Harberts Road with Helions Road. (Photomatic Ltd.)

The first unwelcome deterioration in the appearance of the post-war classes has arrived by 1955. The wheel trims on RF638 are now painted in place of the original polished finish. The angle of lighting has emphasised the panelling along the vehicle's length and the four quarter drop windows. The vehicle is employed as WY2 on route 437 which then operated between Woking and Weybridge. (Peter Gomm collection)

Western SMT fleet number GY993, which was originally London Transport's G400, passes the Gourock tram depot on 30th July. Disposed by the Executive in December 1951 it received this new Alexander lowbridge body, number 4276, in December 1952. Eighteen other ex-London Guy's were similarly involved in this rebodying programme at the same time. (J.C.Gillham)

STD44 after its years pounding the streets of London found itself in much quieter Royal Leamington Spa working for Priory Garages and Coaches Ltd. Except for a complete external repaint, the addition of a driver's cab door and the removal of garage and duty running number brackets, the bus appears much as it would have when first entering service with the Board in May 1937 with both upper and lower deck window surrounds painted in the relief colour. The rear end of a coach belonging to the same operator manages just to be included in the right of the picture while above the railway arches a semaphore signal confirms the operating base to be adjacent to the railway. (N.Anscombe collection)

RT4265, a Norwood garaged bus, is seen in a deserted Battersea Park on Saturday the 14th May operating as N32 on the Sloane Square and Festival Gardens route 137A, having recently returned to service after its first overhaul. The inspector sent to control the hoards of passengers has turned up his collar and sought refuge from the elements on the platform of the bus. (A.G.Newman)

RF20 received its first overhaul in February of the year under review appearing in this drab revised livery into which all the original superbly finished green and grey private hire batch of twenty five vehicles were painted by the end of the year. The coach still carries a London Transport fleet name but after conversion along with all of the batch from RF15 to RF25 for regular Green Line work in 1956, would carry a fleet name more suited to its new role. Operating from Northfleet, the coach is pictured outside Windsor garage with a good load of passengers boarding on 1st August. (A.B.Cross)

STL2682 stands at the Broxbourne Station bus stop on 21st May while on its way from Nazeing to Hertford on route 327 as duty HG36 just days before being withdrawn from service and replaced by 2RT2 class vehicles six years its senior. The only alterations made to the exterior of this batch of twenty vehicles during the preceding nine years of operation would appear to be the current all over green livery broken only by the between decks cream band together with the addition of two reflectors low down on the rear panel but not visible from this angle. This particular vehicle was to give another five years service to Widnes Corporation Transport as shown later in this book, eventually passing to that Council's building department for use as a site hut. (J.C.Gillham)

This dusty, unidentifiable 1/4Q4/1 with registration number C4863 was photographed on 30th August at the Place Republik in Belgrade, Yugoslavia. Other than the removal of the life guard rail and the Green Line side board brackets little else has changed on the vehicle since its earlier years with London Transport. Any information on the various London Transport vehicles exported to Yugoslavia would be most welcomed by the author. (J.C.Gillham)

RFW2 is about to enter Victoria coach station to pick up passengers for an afternoon tour of the West End. Behind the coach the British Overseas Airways Corporation building with its symbolic sculpture by E.R.Broadbent is visible. Completed in 1939, the building and its function looms large over the more mundane means of transport offered by its opposite number in Buckingham Palace Road.

In October and November 1954 fifteen spare RT bodies were purchased from Park Royal Coachworks and stored ready for the full RT overhaul programme at Aldenham, which got under way in 1955. This is body 9178 temporarily resting on the chassis of former SRT138, being that which was originally STL2420. It is seen inside New Cross garage before being moved to Aldenham from where it emerged in June mounted on the chassis of RT4140. A similar body from this batch, which was numbered 9172 to 9186, can be seen alongside. Both bodies show a considerable amount of dust accumulated in the months during which they have been standing idle. The addition of NX garage plates seems a little over possessive on the part of the south east London garage. (John Gascoine collection)

RF212 entered service in April 1952 and still resides at Windsor which was its initial allocation. Here it picks up passengers in Windsor before heading over what was later marketed as "The Royal River Route", Green Line 718. The boarding point, number 4, also serves Green Line route 725 to Gravesend and Thames Valley route 20 to Maidenhead and High Wycombe. There cannot be many single stops which serve such widely dispersed destinations. (R.F.Mack)

RT1102 working a short journey on route 351 turns on to the stand at Rickmansworth while the conductor already takes his ease in the time honoured position on the longitudinal seat with his back against the fareboard. (R.H.G.Simpson)

Chalk Farm was a little unusual in running RT, RTL and RTW types simultaneously and in its time route 24 saw all three classes. However, the last four RTs were transferred out in February 1955 leaving it to be an all Leyland garage. Nevertheless occasional loans brought AECs back to route 24 as seen here where Hendon's RT4701 works from Chalk Farm garage at Camden Town. The RT8/2 body built by Weymann at their Addlestone factory together with similar bodies by Park Royal represented the final development of the RT. (J.Gascoine collection)

The Beaconsfield to Gerrards Cross via The Chalfonts route 305 was extended to Uxbridge on 18th May to compensate for reductions on route 455 which operated direct via the A40 from High Wycombe to Uxbridge. RLH46, garaged at Amersham from new in October 1952, received its first overhaul in November of this year and was eventually transferred to Addlestone in May 1956, managing only one summer's operation on the extended route. (R.H.G.Simpson)

Putney Bridge garaged RTW435 in service on route 14 on 20th August passes an unusual background in the shape of St.James' Palace, the name of which comes from an earlier building with a much different purpose. It was a leper hospital dedicated to St.James the Less for the support of which a May Fair was held each year, an event which gave the district its name. The bus has been diverted away from Piccadilly and it will continue past Buckingham Palace and up Constitution Hill to regain its normal route at Hyde Park Corner. Between the taxis on the left of the picture is a lovely MG AZ Magnette first put into production in 1953, while on the extreme right is a Nuffield Oxford taxi. (J.H.Price)

RF334 operates on route 241 to Sidcup garage passing Holy Trinity Church at the junction of Hurst Road and Station Road, Sidcup. This RF bus managed to visit many of the Central Area garages involved in single deck operation during its long life with London Transport which ended when it was withdrawn from service in 1977. It is not one of those preserved nowadays but a number of its contemporaries are to remind us of the classic lines of an AEC Regal Mark IV with Metro-Cammell bodywork. (R.Wellings)

Sometime in August RT3602 and T786 rest within Grays garage yard. The blinds of the RT are set for work on short route 323B between Grays and Fairway which, with the introduction of the Country Area winter programme on 5th October, was extended to Stifford Clays, the service being augmented with the 323A. The pristine condition of the RT is a little odd since the photographer confirms the date as 1955 which ties up with the presence of T786. The RT however was new in 1952 and not overhauled until 1956. Maybe it was a favourite with the staff at Grays garage. (Peter Gulland)

Two of Elmers End's buses are seen being prepared for Bank Holiday duplication work outside Chelsham garage on 30th May. Route 403 paper stickers have been inserted into the front and side route box apertures in readiness for their use on unfamiliar roads. RT844 with RT809 both carry the later style of RT3 bodywork with higher canopies, provision for semaphore trafficator fitment and upswept cutaway above the offside dumb iron. (A.G.Newman)

Route 180 was introduced in October 1951 to operate between Catford garage and Woolwich on a Monday to Saturday basis being a regular replacement for some special journeys hitherto operated by tram services 36 and 38 to and from Lewisham. Operation was by RT type buses from Catford garage and RT1489 is captured on film at the Woolwich, Powis Street stand operating to Lower Sydenham Station to which point the route had been extended in March 1953. The trolleybus wiring for the 696 and 698 terminal can just be seen in the background. (W.Legg)

Green Line RF215 puts in a duty as CM22 on route 464 normally operated by the GS class of vehicle. The bus waits at Oxted on 1st August on a lovely sunny and peaceful Bank Holiday Monday. The background shows the hotch potch of architecture resulting from ad hoc additions to the High Street of a town just inside the County of Surrey and within sight of the North Downs. (J.H.Aston)

RT13 operates on route 28 from Chelverton Road, Putney garage and is parked at the Wandsworth Bridge terminus with RTL1145 further along the road in use on route 91. 1955 was the last year of passenger service for the red liveried members of the first 151 RTs. It was half way through February when the then largest post war reduction of operating schedules took place which allowed these RTs together with the postwar STDs, STLs and G436 to be withdrawn from passenger use. (G.Mead)

This nostalgic picture of RT35 leaving Chiswick Works on learner duties just had to be included in this book to place on record the familiar gates to which many enthusiasts made pilgrimages over many years. On a very wet 5th February the bus emerges before turning left into Chiswick High Road with the famous Chiswick Works bullseye attached to the fencing in the background. The LGOC had brought its central works into use in 1921/22 in order to standardise maintenance of London buses instead of it being carried out at thirty or more garages across London. Now Chiswick Works are no more and the work is carried out by different companies across London. Who says history doesn't run in circles? (G.Mead)

Once STL1472 this bus is now some showman's pride and joy judging by the intricate lining out which has been applied. Some sort of door arrangement has been added to the original front entrance Weymann body but sadly the years have taken their toll and the vehicle is beginning to look very tired. (S.A.Newman)

RT3361 runs alongside the United Dairies milk depot at Vauxhall. This route 69 had commenced operation on 6th January 1952 being part of the sixth stage of the conversion from tram to diesel bus, replacing tram service 54. The route number 69 had lain dormant since 21st April 1943 and it was to be 1958 before the route would be more logically renumbered 36B. (R.Wellings)

To add passenger carrying capacity the Finsbury Park to Alexandra Park short workings on route 233 were double decked on 7th September using RTLs from West Green garage and in this shot RF428 and an RTL share the temporary stand in Clifton Terrace at Finsbury Park. Eventually in 1961 this anti-clockwise operation of the bus terminus on the north side of Finsbury Park Station became permanent but in 1955 it was only a short term expediency. Through working of double deckers on route 233 to Northumberland Park was not possible at this stage due to the low bridge under the Palace Gates branch line in Station Road, Wood Green. (A.D.Packer)

The former STL1853 waits in Drummer Street, Cambridge on 7th May prior to departure on the Premier Travel route to Royston, a journey that will take it through very different surroundings from that of the Blackwall Tunnel for which it was designed. The chassis and body lived happily together from April 1937 when new until February 1960 when the bus was finally scrapped after spending its last years in use as a tree cutter with Premier. (J.C.Gillham)

This was once B9, the last of the first batch of Bristols delivered to the LPTB during the war years, entering service in June 1942. It is seen here rebodied and in totally different surroundings to those of the Ealing and Hanwell area it had experienced until June 1951 when it was withdrawn from London service. Crosville Motor Services of Chester acquired the vehicle in December 1952, rebodied the chassis with this Strachan lowbridge 55 seat body which had originally been carried by FFM315, a 1945 Bristol K6A, and allocated it fleet number MB168. The story does not end there as we shall see in a later volume as the chassis was again rebodied and the bus renumbered. (R.Marshall)

The crew of STL2696 stretch their legs and chat to one another at the picturesque Nazeingwood Common terminus by the pond on 21st May before making a return journey to Hertford on route 327. The bus has very few days left in London service but another nine years work in Dundee lie ahead. These 18STL20s were actually a standard "provincial" type AEC Regent chassis with Weymann 56 seat bodywork and were the last type of the STL class to operate in passenger service with the Executive, although these twenty vehicles bore little affinity to their forbears. The class letters STL first appeared on the streets of London in 1932 and their numbers were added to over the years until in February 1946 the last, the highest being numbered 2701, entered service from Watford High Street garage; a span of some fourteen years. (J.C.Gillham)

RT1402 spent its entire short lived passenger service with LTE from October 1948 through to September 1956 garaged at Watford High Street. Having arrived at the bus stop in Watford town centre a small crowd now board for the journey which will take the bus as far as Oxhey Estate, Hallows Crescent. The bus was to find further service with the Ayrshire Bus Owners (A1 Service) of Ardrossan in Scotland from July 1957, having been initially sold to Birds Commercial Motors of Stratford Upon Avon in September 1956. (A.B.Cross)

The handy parking area alongside Victoria garage which for a while in later years was referred to as "Wilton Road Coach Station" is the lay over spot for Old Kent Road garaged RT3999 employed on the circular tour of London, Excursion Number 1. This RT had only recently been transferred from Twickenham garage to its present home only to be further transferred to New Cross in the following year. All the advertisers have stood the test of time and the same products are still available today.

Red liveried RT1509 spent two months garaged at Northfleet, having been one of a number of Craven bodied RTs stored at Stockwell during the early part of the summer. It is seen here in Christianfields Avenue on 25th September operating a duty on the Gravesend and Northfleet local route 495 to Northfleet Church. Again put into store at Stockwell, it was eventually withdrawn from service with London Transport in August 1956 after a further few months in Central Area use. (Lyndon Rowe)

Many ex Q type buses found further service as contractor's vehicles transporting building workers around the different sites which were many in the era of the post-war boom of new housing and factory development. Pictured standing on an unmade road in typical site surroundings ex Q9 is now working for Carlyle (contractors) of Manchester. Only used in this new role from January 1954 until 1956 this 4Q4 was cut up by Salmon and Blair (breakers) of Manchester in February 1957. (Real Photographs Co. Ltd.)

Excursion Number 91, Acton Market to Chorleywood also picking up at Ealing and Greenford, was a new facility introduced in 1955 and was the only one to this spot. The destination was perhaps a little surprising as an excursion objective although there were good walks nearby and if a match was on, cricket to be watched on the Common. RT4717 stands on Chorleywood Common and although official records credit HW with operation, it appears to carry an AC garage plate. Many additional excursions were added to the summer programme during this year taking the number available to well over a hundred, which was quite impressive considering the small beginnings of only a few years previous.
(J.G.S.Smith collection)

Built in 1930, UR6801, an AEC Regal with Harrington bodywork to coach standards entered service with the Lewis Omnibus Company Ltd. of Watford as their fleet number R7. On 1st October 1933 LPTB acquired the business and R7 became T360. Being of long distance and private hire standards the coach together with other similar Lewis vehicles came to be allocated to London Transport's private hire depot at Brixton Hill. In 1938 the vehicle was withdrawn from service and disposed of to Lancashire Motor Traders of Knott Hill in May. After further service with at least two London coach operators, ex-T360 was by April 1950 being used by a showman as living quarters and some five years later on 11th June is pictured basically in its original condition but with some added home comforts. (A.B.Cross)

Once T300 in the LPTB fleet and disposed of by the Board in August 1938, a nearside view of this vehicle appeared in the 1954 book of this series but a further view showing its continued existence in 1955 seemed appropriate. Now carrying coachwork by Duple, the vehicle originally entered service from Tunbridge Wells garage in February 1931 with a Ransome, Sims and Jefferies body.

The public house sign in the background identifies the Packhorse at Gerrards Cross as the resting place for RT3671 which was transferred into Amersham garage a couple of years before its first overhaul in May 1956. The only added brightness in this view taken during the winter months is the Omo advertisement carried along the length of the bus! (B.A.Jenkins)

RTW282 lays over on a short working of route 15 at the Blackwall Tunnel stand before returning to Ladbroke Grove, The Eagle in this view taken in August. Beyond the RTW an RTL on the Isle of Dogs route 56 also basks in the sunshine. (Peter Gulland)

When originally built in 1924, the forecourt of Edgware Underground station was surrounded on three sides by a colonnade and a flower bed occupied the spot where these buses are standing. The flower bed was removed at an early date as buses got bigger and more numerous and the north side was demolished just before the war to make way for the extension of the Northern Line to Bushey Heath. The extension never materialised and it is only recently that the ugly gap and fence seen here has been replaced by buildings which restore the symmetry of Stanley Heaps' neatly designed station. Nearest the camera Edgware's RT2114 waits to operate a short journey on route 107 to Borehamwood although it rather oddly displays a route blind for short journeys at the eastern end of the route. Beyond it RT529 waits to work the northern part of route 142 to Watford Junction. (C.Carter)

GS83 operating from Dorking garage waits in very bleak conditions outside the Plough Inn at the aptly named Coldharbour. The fall of snow has abated for now although the overall lighting conditions suggest more may be on the way. This is an aspect of the delightful Surrey Downs that the summer trippers never see. (F.W.Ivey)

Willesden's RTW425 is pursued by a rather nice post-war Standard 12/14 car as it passes through Harrow on its Sunday journey to London Bridge having commenced its long haul at Edgware. Harrods, the well known London top people's store situated in Brompton Road, used London buses to carry their message over many years as can be verified in this series of books. (Photomatic)

RT145 runs along Clapham Common North Side on its journey to Peckham on 27th May. Although now fitted with full blind display this rear view demonstrates the fact that the rear roof route number box on the 2RT2 class was not brought back into use in post-war years. The front end of an Austin truck nudges into view, probably using the Champion spark plugs advertised on the back of the RT. This type of bus had only a few days left in Central Area passenger service and RT145 would soon find itself stored at Stockwell garage before being given new work as a trainer later in the year. (J.C.Gillham)

The 329A route was a Tuesday and Saturday operation between Datchworth and Hitchin serving the market days in that north Hertfordshire town. The Hertford based vehicle for this route worked out to Knebworth on the 329 route and carried out two return journeys on route 329A, occupying some of its layover time at Hitchin by short runs to Great Wymondley on route 386. After the final 16.30 trip back to Datchworth a short was worked to Nup End followed by a journey back to Hertford on the 329. On Tuesdays these were the only journeys on route 329 but on Saturdays they fitted into a two hourly service on this route except that the final return journey to Hertford was only sixteen minutes behind the normal scheduled journey which must have guaranteed a quiet run indeed. GS12, subsequently preserved, awaits departure from St.Mary's Square, Hitchin. (R.Wellings)

With Windsor bus garage as a backdrop, Tunbridge Wells garage's RF40 stands before departing on the long haul into Central London and back out again to Tunbridge Wells which is a run of well over fifty miles by the route of Green Line 704. Note on the route board the term "London Airport" which was still current for London (Heathrow) in 1955, well before the present confusion of London (Gatwick) not to mention London (Stansted) and London (Luton)! (P.Gomm collection)

RF499 stands in Cromwell Road a little short of the entrance to Kingston garage with blinds already set for its return journey on route 213 to Belmont Station. In a short while it will be manoeuvred through the garage to the bus station section of the building to pick up its passengers. Note that the bus carries the old style of blind which was largely phased out when the new RFs entered service. The Bentalls building in the background was used for storage while the largest of all Kingston retail outlets was situated as now in the centre of the shopping area.

RF592 stands alongside its home garage at Addlestone with the impressive London Transport bullseye mounted above the flat roofed part of the building. At least this garage still exists and the operations have not been transferred to some so called "green field" site so common today and which do not merit such grandiose signs of ownership. The bus has run into the garage on route 462. (Peter Gomm collection)

Having completed its journey to Windsor, RF280 loops round River Street in Royal Windsor, with the outer wall of the castle rising in the background, in order to run back to the garage for its lay over. Now garaged at Northfleet the coach would complete many journeys on this south orbital route, being destined not to be re-allocated until 1960. (John Fozard)

While engaged on a short working of route 410 taking it only as far as Bletchingley, RLH20 stands in the marked out roadway for buses at Reigate. This bus remained at Godstone garage through two overhauls in July 1954 and July 1958 but after its July 1963 visit to Aldenham it moved to Addlestone for two years. It was then stored at various locations for a number of years before finally being disposed of in May 1968. (R.Wellings collection)

Standing in Francis Grove at the old Wimbledon terminus of route 155 on 2nd March, RTL833 presents quite a hazard to any driver wanting to turn left into the road from where the photographer stands. In fact the official stand commenced three yards back from the junction which even so was not ideal, particularly as passengers were allowed to be carried on to the stand, which presumably involved alighting into the roadway. This RTL had arrived at Clapham garage in the previous month after having gained its first overhaul. Prior to this it had been garaged at Chalk Farm since new. (W.Legg)

Craven bodied RT1441, closely followed by a fire engine complete with escape ladders, makes its way to Victoria on route 38 while garaged at Leyton which was to be its last operational base before withdrawal and subsequent storage prior to disposal. Humphrey Bogart, Jennifer Jones and Gina Lollobrigida are starring in the film "Beat the Devil" currently showing within theatreland at Leicester Square. (R.Wellings)

Standing in the yard at the back of Hertford garage in May and keeping RF571 company are at least three of the early RTs including RT137 waiting to go into service on route 327 on 1st June. The 386A route from Hertford to Buntingford via Much Hadham, for which the RF is blinded, was actually garage journeys three days a week by which the Hertford buses reached the remote and sporadic 386 route from Bishops Stortford to Hitchin via Buntingford, part of which still operates today under County Bus colours. (J.G.S.Smith collection)

RF602 waits beside "The Two Brewers" at Chipperfield on route 319 which, although having journeys to Sarratt and Watford, chiefly operated between here and Abbots Langley and Garston garage. The 319 still lays over at this spot today but the vehicle will be a Red Rose minibus, which is a far cry from this imposing crew operated AEC Regal. (R.Wellings)

A number of passengers have availed themselves of a seat inside RF585 while it stands in the terminus at St.Mary's Square, Hitchin before commencing its journey to Luton, Park Square via the villages of Kings Walden and Tea Green. The more direct route between the two towns, using the A505, lay to the north of the London Transport area and in 1955 was the province of United Counties. (Peter Gomm collection)

Standing in the corner of Chelsham garage GS1 awaits further use on 2nd July. It was in October 1953 that this bus was first used by the Executive as a trainer at the same garage, going into regular passenger service soon after. After withdrawal from its useful life late in 1962 it was sold in March 1963. It can still be seen nowadays turning up at many rallies in immaculate condition since being acquired by the Model Road and Rail retail shop owners of Worcester Park. (J.H.Aston)

In 1955 a few of the post-war all Leyland STD vehicles managed to acquire a full set of route information blinds before the last of these fine looking buses were withdrawn from service in March. Very few pictures exist of these like this but it is a great pity more did not receive this treatment since it greatly enhances their appearance. Loughton's STD137 makes its way to Leytonstone on route 20A from Debden. All of these sixty five vehicles were sold to B.S.E.Company Ltd. of London who were an export agency, which gives rise to the theory that they were all exported to Yugoslavia in due course, though it would appear that nobody has a complete record of their new owners or registration numbers.
(J.G.S.Smith collection)

RF662 has its two compressed air operated glider type doors in the closed position while it is parked on the offside of the road in Dorking. The blinds are set for route 412 to Holmbury St.Mary (Sutton) which is an odd way of describing two adjacent villages, the Volunteer public house at Sutton being the ultimate destination. Allegedly this was to avoid confusing passengers who wished to travel to the more well known Sutton served by the 470 and the Green Line routes from Dorking. On 5th October the route lost its journeys which bifurcated to Leith Hill, Leylands Road. (Peter Gomm collection)

The driver-conductor of GS57 can just be seen talking to one of his few passengers while another eyes the cameraman as the bus stands at Hartley Court on route 490 which operated between Hartley Court and Singlewell via New Barn and Gravesend. On 5th October the route would be cut back to Gravesend severing the little used through link to Singlewell. (D.T.Rowe)

The Forest Hill terminus of route 124 provides the resting place in October for Catford garaged RT1503. The different rear end treatment of the Craven bodied product when compared to other members of the RT family is evident. To mention but a few, the upper deck shallower rear emergency window with unorthodox opening arrangement and stops affixed either side of the standard route blind apertures are most noticeable. These stops were similar to those fitted to the Leyland built RTW vehicles and precluded the possibility of placing advertisements next to the blind boxes. In the case of the Craven bodies the curved rear profile prevented them being placed outside the stops although this was possible on the RTWs. The much smaller rear window to the platform area provides another distinctive feature and the number plate and rear light cluster are equally distinctive being placed nearer the corner of the body although being to standard LTE requirements. (Peter Gulland)

RTL1020 on route 189A is about to pull away from the kerb outside Clapham South Underground Station in Nightingale Lane on its journey to Raynes Park. The main A24 London to Worthing road can be seen in the background with a hospital across the road which the author remembers always seemed to have a TF ambulance parked in its grounds during the war years, which gives an unfortunate insight into his age! (R.Wellings collection)

The date is 3rd September and in crowded conditions RTL1209, operating from Willesden garage on route 46 leads RT3765 past the Victoria Palace on its way from Waterloo to Alperton, the extreme destination of the route despite the admonition "Only" on the ultimate blind. The RT behind is a little shy at showing the route number of the service it operates on though it is making its way to Chelsea Bridge Road on route 39. The J.Lyons & Co.Ltd. teashop in the background was a regular meeting place at one time on Saturday evenings for London Transport enthusiasts who used to swop notes of their day's observations over beans on toast in the era before LOTS served all the information up on a plate! (A.B.Cross)

Southall garage gained two RTs with the changes introduced on 12th October involving routes 120 and 120A and the introduction of new route 232. RT3570 is pictured at the new Hounslow garage bus station before departing to operate as duty HW189 to Greenford, Civil Engineer. (R.H.G.Simpson)

This interior view of a Mann Egerton T13 type body with seating for 31 passengers shows the pleasant airy effect achieved by the bodybuilders. The seating is of Accles and Pollock standard tubular make with semi circular hand grips at the top on the gangway side. A bell cord is fitted along the offside length with an additional "push once" bell with a highlighting arrow fixed to the panel near the sliding door. Central winding mechanism is provided for the opening windows and the colour scheme for the interior changes midway up window level in RT style. A fare chart is carried centrally fitted to the front bulkhead and the one depicted here covers route 374, whereon T797 could be found since its transfer to Grays the previous year until its eventual withdrawal from service in 1959. (J.Pilgrim)

Although not needing low height vehicles, the short 415 route between Ockham, Ripley and Guildford often played host to RLH class buses and on a warm summer's day RLH30 proceeds to Guildford flanked by two deliciously vintage looking cars. (D.A.Ruddom collection)

If one disregards the fact that RT934 spent its first year at Sidcup garage in 1948, it was not until March of the year under review that the RT class operated from this south eastern garage. The RTLs which had monopolised double deck operation from Sidcup since late 1948 were gradually ousted by the AECs during April. RT3975, one of the first to arrive, waits on duty SP4 at Finsbury Square on route 21 before departing for a journey over the full length of the route to the Bull at Farningham. (Lens of Sutton)

The railway station at Nish in the Serbian Republic of Yugoslavia provides the resting place for ex-LT1098 on 1st September. Operated by Nish Tramways as their number 12 it is seen in use on route 3, indicated by the makeshift sticker in the driver's window. Amazingly a lot of time and energy has been spent in adding a new doorway to the offside of the saloon on this bus which first entered service in June 1931. With only a limited life expectancy, judging by the front dome and cab area which appear to have broken away from the rest of the body, one might be forgiven for asking was it worth all the trouble. (J.C.Gillham)

GS34 began its operating life at Amersham in December 1953. Routes 348, 373, 397 and 398 were all converted during that month and in 1955 this one man operated bus still plies the Buckinghamshire lanes as it makes its way on the 398 to Quill Hall Estate, which is situated on the north eastern extremities of Amersham. (Michael Rooum)

The Sutton Coldfield Old Peoples' Welfare Committee were the proud owners of ex-Q83 for around ten years from January 1954 until they presented the vehicle to the local St.John's Ambulance Brigade. The bus, a Birmingham Railway Carriage and Wagon Company 37 seat bodied 4Q4, had initially entered service with LPTB in October 1935 operating from Dorking garage in the Country Area. In 1937 it was converted to Green Line use receiving the classification 1/4Q4/1 which reflected the various alterations that had been carried out to fit it for its new role. In 1938 however the coach reverted back to bus work again in the Country Area. It continued its service with London Transport in this capacity finally ending its days allocated to Northfleet before being put into store at Reigate prior to being disposed. Thankfully the vehicle is now preserved, helped probably by its use with the Committee and the staff at the BMMO garage at Sutton Coldfield who serviced and garaged the orange and cream liveried vehicle. (R.F.Mack)

Route 383 was officially allocated one GS plus an additional bus for a weekday morning short journey from Walsworth into Hitchin. It was not until some years later that RFs were allocated by which time Hitchin garage was no more and the operation was based at Stevenage. RF581 however carries a route 383 display and the running number HN101 which suggests it is fulfilling a relief schedule. The more normal bus for the route is GS8 which is parked beyond the RF. (R.H.G.Simpson)

The previously open aspect of the bus terminus at Uxbridge Station is beginning to be destroyed by office building during August as T750 attracts a small number of passengers for its next duty on route 224A to West Drayton, Mill Road. 224A commenced operation on 16th February being the renumbered single deck operated section of route 223. (Peter Gulland)

The second prototype RM in flat grey primer leaves Staines garage on 29th June. London Transport's only new bus in 1955, it was during the first half of March that the bus had been officially taken into stock. It then spent time at Northolt Airport for fuel and performance tests to be carried out comparative to RM1. This was followed by further jaunts, firstly to the MIRA at Nuneaton, then hill climbing and restarting tests at Titsey Hill, a return visit to Nuneaton followed by endurance tests at Chobham (where they test tanks!). It was while at the last mentioned test area that it had called into Staines for refuelling. It is still nearly two years away from entering service on routes 406/406A from Reigate garage by which time a number of major and minor improvements were incorporated resulting from the experience gained in its continuous test condition. (A.B.Cross)

Uxbridge garaged T759 in company with an RT on route 91 stands outside Hounslow West Underground station. The route blinds of the AEC Regal demonstrate the new style which began to appear during 1955 although the unusual treatment of the HOUNSLOW CENTRAL STATION destination looks very untidy. Note also the thicker, smaller numbers used for the route number.

RT133 was the last red liveried of the so called "pre-war" RTs to operate in passenger service, albeit in the Country Area. It is pictured here in August with a small number of passengers as the driver clambers into the cab to commence a journey through to Hertford by way of route 350 from Bishops Stortford. For some reason no HG or running number plates are carried. Officially the bus was a staff bus but acted as an additional spare for one month only to back up its green painted counterparts for the route 327 operation. In September it was recorded as unlicensed at New Cross garage.

The various roof sections are now joined and sealed to a much improved standard compared to that shown by the general view which was taken at Victoria Station forecourt and which appears on page 81 of the 1953 book of this series. This high level view of Northfleet's RT2261 working through to Erith on route 480 has caught the bus turning out of Market Street into Lowfield Street in Dartford, an impossible manoeuvre in the modern day pedestrianisation of this area. (Lens of Sutton)

It is delivery day for rebodied ex-Daimler D18, now carrying a new Harkness Coachworks highbridge body, as it stands outside the coachbuilder's works in Belfast. One hundred of the disposed D class vehicles were similarly treated for Belfast Corporation making them the largest operator of this ex-London class. (W.Montgomery)

RFs 677-682 were new to Crawley garage in October 1953 and here RF680 works on route 473 which ran across the south of the Country Area between Edenbridge in Kent and Horsham in Sussex via Crawley in Surrey. (Surfleet Transport Photographs)

RF571 is seen at the picturesque Nazeing Gate terminus on Tuesday 20th September with the King Harold's Head public house in the distance. The conductor shows his Gibson ticket machine to good advantage and one man operation has yet to arrive. The bus, garaged at Hertford, is operating the single journey on route 342 which travelled beyond Broxbourne to this point to supplement the 327 service. (J.H.Aston)

Although garaged at Dunton Green, RT2264 appears to be working as Green Line relief on the western, London to Windsor, leg of route 705. The canopy blind is set for 704 although the differentiation didn't matter on this part of the joint routes. (J.Gascoine collection)

Daily route 57 commenced operations on 7th January 1951 between Tooting Broadway and Victoria via Streatham as part of the second stage of the post-war tram to diesel bus conversion programme. RT3983 operating from Brixton garage lays over at Streatham on one of the short workings which were all extended on 30th November through to Tooting. The 57 is an interesting route since following changes over the years the previous southern section from Streatham to Tooting is now the northernmost part of the route and it reaches Kingston in the south. (R.Wellings collection)

A number of ex-STLs were operated by the contractor Holland and Hannen and Cubitts on contract to the London County Council in the era around the year under review. STL1626 on the left with STL708 carrying Cubitts' fleet numbers 504 and 509 respectively keep further unknown examples company on 7th April in what appears to be a builder's yard. The buses look remarkably well presented and are a credit to the contractor. (A.B.Cross)

RTL933 was not resident at Wandsworth garage for very long, having moved in after its first overhaul earlier in the year and then moved out long before the end of the following year. Route number 44 came into use again on 1st October 1950 with the first stage of the tram to diesel bus conversion, having laid dormant since 28th October 1941 when ST type buses operated by Holloway and Victoria garages on the then Monday to Saturday service between Victoria and Kings Cross ceased. Here the bus stands on the north side of Lower Green West, one of the three stands available to buses terminating at Mitcham, "The Cricketers", before returning to London Bridge.
(Roy Marshall)

In this July view the ladies wear their mid-calf length dresses while most of the gentlemen are dressed in suits, which is a far cry from today's casual wear attitude. T775, garaged at Two Waters, operates on route 307 as it arrives in Hemel Hempstead on its way from Harpenden to Boxmoor Station. Except for a few months at the end of its operational service with London Transport this bus was always garaged at this Hertfordshire base. The Milk Bar was still common in 1955 before the days of the fast food outlets serving burgers, chips and coke. (R.Wellings)

RF9 was transferred into Reigate garage in March and found use on Green Line duties covering the overhaul of the Green Line coach RFs which got under way in earnest around June of this year. Having had its first overhaul prior to being transferred into RG it wears the new colour scheme of all over green with red fleet names which did nothing for the general appearance of these previously attractive two coloured coaches. Passengers board the southbound coach at Sutton Station on 2nd July. (A.B.Cross)

RTL1117 was the only London Transport owned bus to make a trip over to the Continent during the year under review. It is seen at Chiswick works in May having been prepared for its tour to Holland and carries suitable blinds and makeshift door to the open platform area. (London Transport Museum U57505)

Having just been returned from overhaul, Croydon's RT227 now finds itself operating on a railway replacement service at Purley. This was before the days of "Railway Emergency Service" blinds and a bulkhead slipboard has to suffice. Croydon garage would be the last operational base for this bus as in the last month of 1958 it would be put into storage at Stockwell prior to its sale to Birds in April 1959, still with the body number 1476 as seen here. This bus is now preserved and often attends rallies to remind one of the red RT3 body with low canopy, although the owners have perversely chosen to paint it into the green Country Area livery which it never carried while in LT ownership. (A.G.Newman)

Uninhabited GS 51, with NF57 duty plates and blinds set for a journey on route 450 by the "scenic route" to Dartford via Southfleet Station and Bean, waits at an equally deserted road junction in Gravesend. Alas this particular vehicle escaped being preserved and so cannot join its sisters who still regularly attend rallies around the country.

Now in use as a staff bus, RT118 carries a slip board showing "TWICKENHAM 3" beneath the canopy. The triangle badge fixed to the top of the radiator is interesting as it is not a London Transport standard fixture. Does anyone remember the wording on it and why it was so affixed? (P.Malsher)

A number of transport enthusiasts with interests other than London buses and coaches are catered for in this view of a corner of the Lancashire Motor Traders yard at Salford. With so much British Railways rolling stock in the background not to mention the military type vehicles, one might be forgiven for not focusing on ex-RTC1 straight away. After its initial disposal to W.North of Leeds in March it quickly moved on to its next temporary owner before eventually being used as a staff bus by Vernon Industries Ltd. in Kirkby for no less than five years, although after this reprieve it was ultimately broken up by a dealer named Price of Birkenhead. (John Fozard)

Upton Park's RT1649 leads a column of its stablemates at the Royal Albert Dock terminus (now referred to as Cyprus) of the northern section of the high frequency route 101 on Saturday 21st May. No fewer than 54 buses were allocated to this route by Upton Park on Saturdays in 1955. Various well known manufacturers advertise their products including Air France extolling their Viscount service, long since superseded by the jet era. The crews of the three buses while away their time inside their vehicles being denied a "cuppa" in the otherwise handy establishment which boldly carries a "Closed" sign. (J.H.Aston)

RM1 stands within the South Bank show area of the Aluminium Centenary exhibition held in London between the 1st and 10th June. The date is the 7th and the bus is still in its original form with single small route apertures above the platform and on the rear. Lacking registration number it is squeezed in next to a Jensen passenger chassis. Unladen weight of 6tons, 14cwts, 2lbs for a sixty four seater compares very favourably with the 7tons, 5cwts of a standard fifty six seat 3RT. (A.B.Cross)

Route 726 was introduced on 17th July 1946 to operate as a summer only irregular limited stop service between London and Whipsnade Zoo. In March 1948 the central London terminal was resited from Harewood Avenue, Marylebone to Baker Street Station, Allsop Place and in May 1954 the lengthy garage journeys from Romford were "livened up" by extending the route right through to Romford Market Place. RT3248 pauses at the alighting point at Baker Street Station on a return journey from Whipsnade to Romford. A notice affixed to the bus stop pole also points would-be customers in the direction of where to catch a coach to Whipsnade Zoo. The Victoria Wine Co.Ltd. occupies the premises at 220 Baker Street while in earlier years we are led to believe that Sherlock Holmes resided at number 221B which is actually on the other side of the road. (A.B.Cross)

Originally disposed of to R.L.Daniels, the dealer of Rainham, in October 1949, LT809 was in succeeding years converted to become a heavy mobile crane. It is seen here in the yard of its owners, R.Springfield of Taplow, Bucks on 31st July in company with another interesting but unidentified vehicle in the background. (R.Hobbs/A.B.Cross)

The Westminster Bank Limited building looms above parked GS65 at Chesham Broadway while the seated driver-conductor takes a short break before journeying on after making the necessary route blind adjustments. Route 397 operated between the Broadway and Tring and utilised these small vehicles which had taken over from older C class buses in 1953. (R.H.Simpson)

During the 1950s the 307 and 307A routes had three different terminals at Harpenden, all within a quarter of a mile stretch of Westfield Road. The second and furthest was at Hyde View Road into which the buses reversed and T778 is heading there in this view at the junction of the High Street and Station Road in Harpenden. An RF arrives down Station Road from the Batford direction and no doubt the determined looking ladies are waiting for a 321 to Luton. The public house seen behind the bus once housed much railway memorabilia including many station signs and made a visit well worth while. Unfortunately over the years the contents have been removed and the building now sports a different name.

On a Friday in 1955 T793 could be seen parked at Tring London Transport garage next to an Aylesbury garaged Bristol L, number 351 of the United Counties Omnibus Company. Its Essex registration, ONO999, portrays its origins with Eastern National when that company operated the services in this area prior to May 1952. The 387 was the regular Tring local service but on this particular day of the week the UCOC route 16A operated uniquely from Aylesbury garage between Tring and Long Marston.

The buildings behind RT3873 have now all gone in the name of progress since in the latter months of 1955 work commenced on redeveloping the area and now the University of Luton and its accompanying car parking spaces occupy the site. Route 376, on which the RT has just completed a journey, ran from Kensworth through the lanes around Slip End and Woodside, entering Luton down Farley Hill. (Roy Marshall)

Route 44A was introduced in October 1953 as a Sunday variant of route 44 to run between Mitcham and Charing Cross. RTL933 was transferred into Wandsworth garage after its first overhaul in April of the year under review having previously operated out of Tottenham garage. Wandsworth garage traces its origins back to the horse tram era, subsequently operating both electric trams and trolley-buses and diesel buses in the form of RT class vehicles upon the first stage of the post-war tram conversion programme on 1st October 1950. The RTs were replaced by RTLs within a few months and were to stay until 1967. (W.Legg)

The annual ritual which takes place at Wimbledon during the summer has always required special services to serve (no pun intended!) the All England Lawn Tennis Club grounds. In 1955 services were provided to and from either Wimbledon or Southfields stations and here at the grounds RTL1088 waits for custom before apparently departing for the latter. However, close examination of the London Transport sign in the background shows that buses for Wimbledon depart from this point and the Southfields buses may be found in the opposite direction!

Newly overhauled RT285 stands at the boarding point in Buckingham Palace Road beside Victoria Station for the circular tour of London from Victoria, which in 1955 was known as Excursion Number 1. A number of tourists, who look rather different to the present day riders on the "Round London Tours", have taken advantage of the fine view they can expect from the upper deck. In 1955 Old Kent Road garage was responsible for this prestige operation. (John Fozard)

The new order of things at Putney Bridge garage is demonstrated by RTL1153 which was transferred in during August, adding to the sounds of Leyland engined vehicles in the area. The bus heads across London on the long established 96 route which at one time reached Loughton and had its origins in a pre-first world war National Steam Car Company route. Alas, it was to become a victim of the 1958 cut backs but for the moment it jogs along comfortably to Redbridge Station. (F.W.Ivey)

RT971 works route 310A through to Enfield on 20th September as HG1 and is photographed at Broxbourne. The colourful advertising hoardings probably hide an otherwise untidy area and the Guinness toucan performs its prodigious balancing act. In fact with beer and whisky on the bus and Guinness on the hoarding it is a rather alcoholic picture! (J.H.Aston)

1955 must have been one of those years which enjoyed a reasonable summer judging by the bright sunshine and open windows of both vehicles and housing which is apparent in many of the illustrations to be seen throughout this book. Here on 9th July the driver of GS63 is preoccupied with his passengers who are boarding in Parker Avenue, Bengeo for the journey into town from this one-time village which lies on the B158 road just north of the centre of Hertford to which it is by now contiguous. The old style small Country Area bus stop has definitely seen better days. (A.B.Cross)

Two buses, similar in age but very different in appearance, stop in the centre of Gravesend on 5th August. The lead vehicle, RT995, originally entered service in October 1948 from Northfleet garage where it resided until 1956. The Weymann bodied Bristol K6 following dates from September 1949 and was one of a number of vehicles purchased with this chassis in the early post-war period by Maidstone and District Motor Services Ltd. (J.H.Aston)

Craven bodied RT1424 rests outside Windsor garage complete with crew taking advantage of the longitudinal seating in the lower saloon before commencing a journey to London as Green Line relief WR134 on Bank Holiday Monday, 1st August. The body manufactured by this Sheffield based organisation was one of twenty seven always painted in the Country Area livery during their comparatively short stay with the Executive. (A.B.Cross)

One man operated CR34 entered service in December 1939 from Uxbridge garage being used on routes 223 and 224 replacing older DA class vehicles. The bus together with the other members of the class were stored during much of the war years, reappearing largely in the capacity of relief vehicles soon after hostilities ended. In June 1949 CR34 was withdrawn from service and eventually disposed of to L.W.Vass the dealer of Ampthill. On 31st July 1955 it is seen in use as a workmen's rest hut at Colnbrook.
(Roy Hobbs)

Routes 410 and 409 met at Godstone and here RLH37 makes for Bromley North Station while East Grinstead garaged RT3147 also journeys northwards but in this instance to West Croydon. The gathering of cars in the background may demonstrate that drinking and driving was still socially acceptable in 1955 and the local Westerham Ales are being sampled. (C.Carter)

London Airport became the top excursion attraction in 1955 and here in the open expanse of the "Central Enclosure" a small convoy of vehicles deposit their passengers for what looks like an enjoyable day. Although the weather is fine and warm as indicated by the many open windows on the buses, some people never feel properly dressed without their top coats. RT476 which has brought the would-be plane spotters from Leyton, leads the line of shiny vehicles. (J.Mitchell)

Route 852 was introduced on 22nd December 1954 at very short notice when F.H.Kilner (Transport) Ltd., one of the B.S.Williams companies, went into liquidation. The London Transport replacement 852 ran between Three Bridges, Crawley and Ewhurst on a short term licence and involved work outside the London Transport area. On 18th May 1955 the route was withdrawn between Horsham and Ewhurst and that section replaced by a service operated by Brown Motor Services of Forest Green. Here, before the cut back, GS81 operates a journey from Ewhurst to Crawley as CY25 with the driver-conductor making sure he can be recognised by future generations. (John Lines collection)

The former Q31, whose last operating territory was the Dunton Green area of the Kent countryside, now finds itself in totally different surroundings on the Mediterranean island of Cyprus. The first letter of its new 1954 registration number indicates its use as a public service vehicle but who with remains a mystery. A couple of British built cars in the shape of a Ford Zephyr Six and a very tired looking Rover are parked further along the road.

Two vehicles made redundant during the year were STL2690 and STD140 which are seen at Chiswick Works on 26th April. The STL, which was the first of its batch to be withdrawn two months ahead of the rest, would be despatched to W.North in July to be sold on to Dundee Corporation the following month. One of ten acquired by this Scottish operator, it was given fleet number 174 by its new owners. The STD was almost certainly exported to Yugoslavia. (J.C.Gillham)

A reminder of the newer section of the former Uxbridge garage which was situated on the Oxford Road, now A4020, just north of the town beyond the Grand Union Canal bridge. Nowadays a new office block stands on the site. The garage was closed with the opening of the present premises adjacent to Uxbridge Underground station. A nicely presented line up of RTs includes from left to right, 3686, 2127, 1868, 3007, 2788, 3703, 773, 1156 and 3006. T757 stands alone opposite the two unidentifiable RTs. (London Transport Museum 13838)

This junction of the A404 with the A412 across the road from Rickmansworth railway station is much changed but the Victoria Hotel still stands although somewhat altered and is now known as The Long Island Bar & Diner. RT4478 climbs the small incline from beneath the railway bridge which crosses the main A412 road to Uxbridge and Slough. Although green, this RT originally entered service in the early part of 1954 from Twickenham garage, moving into the Country Area a few months later. The Park Royal body was originally mounted on SRT69 and upon the vehicle's first overhaul in February 1958 it would be outshopped from Aldenham in Central Area colours.

RT283 executes the awkward U-turn in Vauxhall Bridge Road which was the terminal arrangement for several of the Victoria tram replacement routes for some years. The haphazard way in which this was carried out is demonstrated by the fact that this bus has missed the actual departure stop outside the Cameo Hotel by several yards. The large Woolworth's store in the background had a rear entrance in Wilton Road which was a useful cut through on wet days to get to the railway station. (R.Wellings collection)

GS41 operates as EP13 on route 393, which ran between Hoddesdon and Harlow. Originally entering service from Dorking garage in November 1953 the bus is here picking up passengers at Broxbourne on 20th September. Sadly this vehicle is not one of the members of the class now preserved. (J.H.Aston)

RT20 was one of the first batch of 2RT2s to be put into service in January 1940. Fifteen years on and now wearing the latest colour scheme with correctly finished wheel trims and a complement of full blinds, the bus looks totally undated. A fine tribute to the LPTB design team resident at Chiswick Works who first envisaged this body in 1935 with assistance from the chassis manufacturer. The date is 16th April and the varied architectural background belongs to the town centre of Richmond. (G.Mead)

RT1425 waits at the Uxbridge terminus of route 457A before departing for Windsor Castle on 2nd September. With less than eight months service remaining with the Executive, the bus would be operating much further north before the next twelve months are out. (A.G.Newman)

Several of the Q type of bus found their way to Cyprus in the early 50s and here, operated by the Famagusta Bus Service, is Q158. Although it has the lower front panel removed which holds its Cypriot registration number, TL249, it is still identifiable by the owner's fleet number 10 painted on the nearside corner panel of the roof. The strategically placed lifting gear suggests that the engine may be about to be removed for some sort of attention.

Green Line relief RT3676 operating from Crawley garage heads for London on route 710 showing a rather uninformative destination which could cover a multitude of possibilities. The passengers are obviously more used to the normal RF coach since none have ventured on to the upper deck. It is hard to remember when Boots the Chemist operated such intimate retail outlets as that by the bus stop. (G.A.Rixon)

A heavy tree pruning exercise is in progress which has resulted in the need for two "Tree Pruning Equipment" vehicles to be used. 972J leads 969J, both of which started life as front entrance STLs, numbers 1494 and 1503 respectively. They were converted for their new role in the 1952/53 era and carried on these duties until both were withdrawn in September 1963. (Omnibus Society)

This interesting panoramic view is taken at the Lancashire Motor Traders' yard in Salford. Two TFs, the foremost of which is TF82, still carrying its St.Albans garage blinds, an unidentifiable 10T10 type coach and RTC1, which is at the back by the railway sidings, all of which were originally operated by London Transport. The TFs and RTC1 had arrived during the year under review via W.North of Leeds who acquired all members of the TF class when they were disposed of by the Executive. The T class vehicle is probably one of a number which were received direct from London in the latter months of 1954. In 1956 TF82 was noted as a site office at the Partington power station.

A Standard Vanguard Mark I is about to overtake RT3797 operating on Excursion Number 55 from Enfield to Hampton Court. Enfield garage provided the necessary vehicle for this popular destination from its home town. The location of this picture has eluded us although it is likely to be somewhere in the Teddington area. The Gothic looking residence, reminiscent of the Addams Family is in the throes of demolition. (J.G.S.Smith collection)

RTL1238 is engaged on a Ramblers' Association Excursion identified by W38 in the window beneath the canopy. These excursions, which were very popular, were operated in conjunction with "Fieldfare" of the Evening News who contributed a weekly ramble in that newspaper. They ran on Sundays to various destinations which varied from week to week up to a maximum of eighteen on any one Sunday. (D.A.Jones)

Green liveried RT36 photographed on 20th September at Nazeingwood Common together with a nostalgic road direction sign belonging to the Parish of Nazeing as proclaimed at the top of the post. Before the laying of so many telephone cables underground, well laden telegraph poles such as that behind the bus were a common sight all over the country. Once the required strengthening work had been carried out on the bridge at Broxbourne these 2RT2s were replaced by post-war RTs but this was not to be until 1st September 1957. (J.H.Aston)

Although in later years Wandsworth garage became a daily operator of route 28, in 1955 their involvement was still restricted to a Sunday allocation. Here RTL1167 spends part of its Sabbath on the cobbles of Golders Green Station forecourt. This is early in the year, since the following vehicle is an RT from Middle Row garage which was converted to RTL starting in April. (J.Gascoine collection)

RF3 now wears a drab all over green paint scheme having lost its attractive grey upper panels but it has acquired a semaphore arm trafficator. It is thought this may be Kew Green and the coach awaits its footsore passengers after their visit to the famous gardens.

T791 operated out of Amersham garage from June 1954 until it was withdrawn from service in August 1956. The 15T13s were used as Green Line reliefs from various Country Area garages from time to time and at an unknown date in 1955 this fine looking Mann Egerton bodied bus stands outside MA garage showing blinds for such a duty. (A.B.Cross)

A further vehicle which is preserved and can be seen at the Cobham Bus Museum is "Tree Pruning Equipment" 971J, alias STL1470. It originally entered service in November 1936 being an AEC Regent with a metal framed 48 seat front entrance body designed by London Transport and built by Weymann. Much of the original bodywork of the lower deck has been retained although the blind boxes have been panelled over as have most of the windows in the passenger saloon. The upper deck has been cleared of seats giving access to the offending trees and space to carry the lopped branches. A drop down portion is neatly incorporated towards the back of the vehicle to sweep out the debris. (J.Gascoine collection)

Rye Lane's RT3380 now carries an RT3 body in place of the RT8/2 originally fitted when it entered service with LTE in 1951. The route number 69 had been resurrected to replace tram service 54 in January 1952 having last been used on 20th April 1943 and now operates between Victoria and Grove Park Station where it is pictured. The "News of the World" newspaper still to this day carries on its tradition of reporting on the subject of love in all its guises. (W.Legg)

Overhauled and allocated to Thornton Heath garage at the beginning of 1955, this picture of RT243 had to be included if only for the amusing advertisement carried along its offside. In the present days of truthfulness in advertising one wonders if Guinness really imparts such strength! The location is the entrance to Thornton Heath garage and it is a scene which could be witnessed from 1951 when the garage first opened with two tram replacement routes 109 and 190 until RMs replaced the RTs on this route twenty five years later in October 1976. (W.Legg)

The highest numbered Craven bodied RT was RT1521 and in its final years in service with LTE was garaged at Leyton. It had gained an overhaul in January 1954 and must have represented a bargain to the authorities of Dundee Corporation Transport Department when they were able to acquire it in August 1956. Here in 1955 it leaves Victoria on route 10 bound for Woodford Bridge. A Leyland lorry pulls out of Allington Street while a policeman on point duty controls the busy junction with Vauxhall Bridge Road. Is the tanker really full of beer? (J.Gascoine collection)

RT3644 appears to be waiting to make its return journey from Hampton Court to New Cross Gate once the vehicle has its full complement of passengers. The driver and conductor look in opposite directions for the last few stragglers who are perhaps caught up in the famous Hampton Court maze. (D.A.Jones)

General Gordon Place in the centre of Woolwich, which rose to fame as a bus terminal when the trams were withdrawn, is the location of RT140. The bus finished its temporary duties training tram drivers in 1952 and then returned to passenger service from New Cross, which had been the largest tram depot of all. The vehicle was disposed of before the end of the year under review but here it works route 182, the replacement for tram service 46. (G.Mead)

Part of the town centre of Nish, which is now in the Serbian Republic of the former Yugoslavia, provides the backdrop to a former single deck LT. Operating for Nish Tramways, the unmistakable shape of LT1028, now re-registered C5566 from its previous GO629, makes a sad sight in its neglected state. Gone is the one nearside front exit it had in London in favour of an exit doorway directly opposite where the older one was placed with the former centre rear emergency exit being used for boarding. The bus appears to have lost its engine side cover and the paintwork along the length of the bus has deteriorated to such an extent that it could be operating in bare metal. It also looks as if the seating may have been removed from around the centre portion of the body making the bus an early standee type. (J.C.Gillham)

Croydon garaged RT957 makes its way along London Road en-route from Chipstead Valley to West Hampstead on Sunday service 59, while a 130 heads in the opposite direction from Streatham Common to New Addington. A Morris Minor is about to overtake the 130 but very little other traffic is about. The road resurfacing following the lifting of the tram tracks can be discerned under the 59's front offside wheel. (Roy Marshall)

Route 421, which required one bus, was converted from RF to RT operation with the summer programme introduced in May of the year under review. Red liveried RT1497, brought out of store from Stockwell garage, operated from Dunton Green for a month during the summer and works the upseated service before again finding itself in store at the reinforced concrete structure of Stockwell to gather dust before its next call to duty in 1956. (Surfleet Transport Photographs)

RF217 carries the new style of Green Line blind layout introduced during the year and is seen at Oxted on 1st August. The coach spent its first years at Chelsham garage moving over to Tring after its first overhaul in June 1956. The town and its garage would have already been known to this thirty nine seater as route 707 was jointly operated by the two garages. (J.H.Aston)

From left to right RT52 and RT61 await further use within the confines of Chelverton Road, Putney garage. The building was originally used in the days of horse travel, changing over to motorbus operation in 1912. Extensions and modernisation took place in 1935 and 1936 and it is in this condition that the building is viewed with the buses parked on to the outer wall. The two RTs had both first arrived at the garage in 1940 being part of the large second batch to go into public service in March of that year but now in a few weeks time they would be in store at Stockwell, their passenger carrying days over.

A further route to lose its occasional operation by 2RT2 type buses in 1955 was the 179. Here New Cross garage's RT121, one of the small number fitted with quarter drop opening windows, stands at the Farringdon Street terminus before returning south to Grove Park Station. The bus was eventually disposed of to F.Ridler, dealers of London, in July 1963 after a career with London Transport which lasted from April 1941 when it first appeared on the road from Putney Bridge garage. It carries its original body, numbered 383 in the new series introduced by LPTB in 1939 commencing with body number 1 on a TF coach of the production batch. (J.Gascoine collection)

Former Q60, when in the ownership of Ormac (Contractors) Ltd., is seen on what is now Bishops Rise, South Hatfield in the summer of 1955 during the period the new town was being built. The vehicle was sold to F.Cowley (dealers) of Salford, Lancs in August 1953 by LTE along with a small number of other 4Q4s many of which saw further service mostly in similar capacities to this vehicle. (P.J.Malsher)

RT3763 being overtaken by a speeding Vauxhall car while both make their way along the seedier end of Shaftesbury Avenue. Although severely truncated at its northern end, Route 38 still covers the southern section between Clapton and Victoria as it did when first introduced in 1912, give or take a few one-way traffic schemes. (R.Wellings)

Red liveried RT1489 works duty WR38 on the Slough town route 446. This bus had been transferred into the Country Area during July at first to provide Addlestone garage with vehicle cover for the Ascot races. Its previous Central Area home had been Alperton and in October it was back on more central duties initially at Holloway. Its rather short life with the Executive lasted from November 1949 through till April 1957 to be supplemented with an even shorter one with the Ayrshire Bus Owners (A1 Services) which ended following an accident.

A busy thoroughfare with a choice of architecture styles as a background together with trolleybus wiring casting shadows make an interesting view as RTL967 heads up Pentonville Road. Operating from Chelverton Road, Putney garage and having commenced its journey at Roehampton, the bus doesn't have too far to go before it reaches its final destination at Hackney Wick.

T463, once registered ELP187, now carries Serbian registration number C2579 in this view taken on 29th August. Some interesting modifications have been made to the LPTB built body, not least being the new exit doorway built into the old offside. A handy, if not too user friendly, metal framed two tier step is attached to the rear to allow boarding through the old emergency exit although there is still a fairly high step up from the roadway needed to ascend into the saloon. The bus is parked on the Place Republik in Belgrade, Yugoslavia. (J.C.Gillham)

Route 247A received its usual summer extension from Collier Row to Chigwell Row in 1955 and RT2351 operates through Romford to the Harold Hill Estate with Barking's RTL545 following behind. Interestingly, cigarette tobacco was the princely sum of 3/8d per ounce in those far off days. (W.J.Haynes)

Crawley garaged T787 passes through Horley on 10th July while employed on route 426 which operated on a circular route from Crawley. A number of these Mann Egerton bodied Ts found their way to this southern Country Area garage from Garston in the middle of 1953 when a sizeable allocation of country bus RFs were delivered to the latter. (R.Hobbs/A.B.Cross)

RT2775 followed by a Vauxhall Velox or Wyvern gets the red and amber signal to allow it to cross into Richmond Road under the Kingston railway bridge. The bus has just left its terminal stand in the Bus Station and after meandering through Ham to Richmond will head up over Chiswick Bridge to Hammersmith where it will terminate at Brook Green. The date is 29th January and the Robertson Golly is still socially acceptable. The GB plate proclaims the RT's previous ventures abroad which took place in 1952. (A.B.Cross)

Passing over Putney Bridge in the early evening gloom on 29th March, RTL1064 heads south into Putney High Street on its way to Kingston while Forest Gate's RT1796 prepares to turn right into Lower Richmond Road as it nears the end of its long journey from Redbridge. 1955 was before the era of flashing trafficators and the Forest Gate driver gives a clear hand signal to indicate his intentions. (A.B.Cross)

STDs 140 and 167 await their fate, stored within the reconstructed Shepherds Bush garage. It is believed the entire batch of these all Leyland products numbering sixty five, which were only nine years old, were eventually exported to Yugoslavia. Close examination reveals that STD140 was one of the few vehicles in the class which at the end utilized the full front blind display. Many of these buses were photographed in their new surroundings as will be seen in this and future books of the series. (John Gascoine collection)

What was once STD32 in the London Transport fleet is now Garner's Buses (Bridge of Weir) Ltd. of Renfrewshire fleet number 27. This all Leyland product comprises a chassis model TD4 with 56 seat highbridge bodywork. It first entered service in May 1937 from Hendon garage where it resided until being withdrawn from service in December 1953 to spend four more years with its new operators. (N.Anscombe collection)

GS30 stands half in and half out of the shadows of Guildford garage on 2nd July while stablemates RF96 and RF278, both in Green Line livery, together with a Country bus RF and an RLH rest further within the well lit building. Five of this small class of buses with Guy chassis, Perkins engine and ECW 26 seat bodywork were allocated to the garage for many years. This example is ready to put in a duty as GF8 on route 448A, which was an in-town offshoot of the main 448 route serving Pewley Way at Charlotteville. (J.H.Aston)

Grantham bus station provides the resting place for a Bristol K6A with Duple bodywork which was once B11 in the London Transport fleet. The bus was operated by the Lincolnshire Road Car Company between April 1953 and July 1960 and here on 18th June it carries its second fleet number with its new operator, No.2107 having originally been known as 993. This vehicle, unlike some others, retained its original body throughout its life. (J.C.Gillham)

The date is 12th February and at bus-busy Woolwich the subject of the camera, RT56, looks superb as it carries a full set of route blinds for its use on route 186 to Crystal Palace. The third bus, standing behind the van, is operating on route 89A which replaced the short lived Woolwich to Shooters Hill route 256 on 5th January running beyond Shooters Hill over the 89 roads to Lewisham. It is one of those routes which seems to have escaped the attention of photographers. (G.Mead)

Ex-STL2343 was used as a showman's vehicle for a number of years after its disposal by the Executive in May 1950. The removal and rebuilding of the rearmost portion has left its last London offside advertisement lacking the C to Crawfords. The exhaust system has been extended to discharge at the upper deck level to which the original LPTB body has been reduced. The smart looking enthusiast (no anoraks here!) records the details in his notebook. (D.A.Jones)

RF276 operates on the additional half hourly service of Green Line route 725 introduced between Windsor and Dartford (Market Street) from 28th April 1954. The route had been inaugurated on 1st July 1953 on an hourly basis through to Gravesend and proved such a success that this augmentation was called for. Note the route board which is dedicated to the shorter workings. This particular RF was transferred into Dartford garage with a small number of others for its involvement on the route which re-introduced Green Line work to this garage for the first time since 1935 when it lost its workings on routes A1/A2. (Lens of Sutton)

RT130 waits on the small incline of Medfield Street at Roehampton before continuing to the bottom and turning to climb up the hill on the next trip to Hackney Wick on route 30. Note the advertisement for the "gay resort of the Festival Gardens and Fun Fair at Battersea Park." This was long before another connotation was put on the word gay. The date is 21st May just four days before the last official day of operation of this sub-class at Chelverton Road, Putney garage. (J.C.Gillham)

Ex-service vehicle 30H, a mobile staff canteen, was originally solid tyred, open top with open driver's cab, red liveried NS250. In March 1954 it was disposed of by the Executive and then found further use as a caravan thirty two years after first entering passenger service from Palmers Green garage. Sadly it does not appear to have much more life left judging by the general appearance of the bodywork although the front nearside tyre has plenty of tread left on it. (D.Jones)

There is something about the angle from which this picture is taken that makes you think you might be looking at an RTW. Appearances are deceptive however and it is the normal 7'6" wide RTL524 which forms part of Dalston's normal allocation to route 78. Indeed it is doubtful if 8' wide vehicles were approved for operation over Tower Bridge at this stage. Route 78 is another stable route number in the London Transport series, first operating between Shoreditch Church, where this picture is taken, and Dulwich on 2nd March 1913 replacing a Tilling horse bus service. At various stages it has reached Finsbury Park in the north and Bromley Common then West Wickham and Croydon Airport in the south but its core Shoreditch to Dulwich section has survived to this day. (W.J.Haynes)

Green Line RT3232 stands in Aldgate Minories bus station with raised motif and in nicely turned out condition except for the rear wheel covers, commonly known as "dustbin lids" by garage engineering staff, which have succumbed to all over green paint. This is the RT which has survived in East London and is currently owned by London Pride Sightseeing. At one time, when in the Ensignbus fleet it was a regular performer on special occasions on their various tendered routes. Various other RT family class vehicles wait for their call to duty including RTW119 in use on route 15 and ready to depart for Ladbroke Grove.

Merton garage was the home of RF370 from new in October 1952 until it was returned to service after its first overhaul in May 1957 to Old Kent Road garage. The bus is working route 200 which started life in September 1930 as 103 being renumbered in October 1934 and which still exists in part sixty years later. (J.Gascoine collection)

Parked with some of her sisters at Garston garage, STL2695 is one of the quarter of this batch of twenty vehicles which served the Watford area to the end of their London Transport lives. Originally all of them were at the former Watford High Street garage, chiefly on routes 321 and 351 but by 1955 town service route 344A was the more likely place these STLs with their distinctive engine sound could be found. In July the whole batch of twenty vehicles would be despatched to W.North the dealer who received many of the retired London vehicles of this era. All these STLs were found new homes with either Dundee, Grimsby or Widnes Corporations. Fortunately one example is preserved to remind us of this interesting variation of the STL series, so numbered for convenience sake since they were so different from their elders. (L.T.P.S.)

PSV Circle publication LT5 quotes STD58 as noted complete in a field near Aylesbury South Station in Buckinghamshire but in a derelict condition. It was during May that this picture of the vehicle was taken but by September the bus had disappeared. Originally disposed of by LTE to W.North's in April of the year under review, it would be interesting to know what led to this superb all-Leyland product being parked here and what were the intentions of the person or persons involved. (J.Gascoine collection)

This rear view of RF281 shows the original Green Line transfer which was carried on the rear emergency door and which was a smaller version of that carried on the side panel. The reflectors fixed to the lower panel have been added sometime after 1954 when this new road traffic safety requirement was first introduced. The coach dates from September 1952 when it first entered service from Dorking garage having been transferred to its present home at Staines in July 1953. Here it is standing beside Windsor garage waiting for the blinds to be changed before journeying over to Gravesend on the orbital route 725 which first ran on 1st July 1953.

Amersham garage played host to a small number of 15T13s which had been transferred in from Garston the previous year and which replaced more elderly 10T10s. T783, being one of the handful, stands alongside the garage in company with a GS and RF both of which remain anonymous. Primarily for use on the 394 group of routes, this T seems to have worked into the garage on route 353 as MA20 and waits for the blinds to be reset, although at least three lady passengers seem to know the next destination as they have already taken their seats. (B.A.Jenkins)

RT64 now performs learner bus duties as it passes along Chiswick High Road at Turnham Green with, on the far side, the old Chiswick Empire where singer Ronnie Carroll tops the bill. No doubt the bus is heading for Chiswick Works and perhaps the driver is a little nervous of his forthcoming appearance on the Chiswick skid patch! (Roy Marshall)

STL2301 strikes a rather undignified pose as it lays on its side on 27th March. It had been withdrawn from service the previous September but was not disposed of until January 1956. The vehicle is a 4/9STL14 and the body taking a bit of a bashing is numbered 17001. (N.Rayfield)

RT3075 passes a small area within Peckham which still awaits the attention of the developers in this view which is only brightened a little by the well presented bus. Operating from Peckham garage the bus carries a chalked on "15" as its running number. The intermediate point blind dates from before the previous year's projection to Crystal Palace although only a small proportion of journeys covered this rail replacement extension from Honor Oak. National Savings advertisements carried both front and side give the bus a dedicated look. (W.Legg)

RT3830 from Kingston garage pauses briefly, possibly for a "comfort stop", at Chelsham garage while on its way to Sevenoaks on Excursion Number 72. This was one of quite a number of new day trips introduced in 1955. In the background an RT complete with route 403 relief blinds soaks up the sun while if you needed a quick cup of tea that facility is ready to hand. (A.M.Wright)

Underneath the Massey built 55 seat lowbridge body number 2137 lurks the chassis of what was once D241 in the London Transport fleet. In 1953 and 1954 Southend Corporation Transport acquired a total of thirteen similar vehicles from the dealer, W.North of Leeds. All were rebodied before entry into service between April and July 1954 and as the intention had been to acquire eighteen vehicles, the overspill of five Massey bodies were fitted instead to the first Leyland Titan buses in the fleet, numbers 276 to 280. If the utility Massey bodies supplied to London Transport had been angular in the extreme, these post-war productions rather went over the top on curves. These Daimlers could be seen on a variety of routes and here on 17th September this example operates route 9A underneath the Southend trolleybus wiring. (A.B.Cross)

Outside Chelsham garage RT1961 and RT3702 bask in the sunshine while inside the building another RT together with a GS are lurking in the shadows. Smartly dressed for impending use as a relief on route 403, red liveried RT1961 is more at home running over the routes allocated to Brixton garage its normal base. A temporary loan to the Country Area for the August Bank Holiday, it was captured on film on Monday, 1st August. (J.H.Aston)

What was formerly STL489 is photographed on 22nd October while in the ownership of the Lancashire Motor Traders Ltd. of Knott Mill. The bus had been withdrawn by London Transport in October 1953 and via a dealer had first seen further service with Morecambe Motors Ltd. of Morecambe from April 1954. A neat driver's door has been added to the otherwise unaltered bodywork as will be confirmed when a comparison is made with the view of the bus in the 1951 book of this series. (J.G.E.Nye)

T794 photographed in the yard at Grays garage in August with sister vehicle T797 standing alongside. Originally delivered to London Transport in September 1948 the buses first saw service from the by now closed Leavesden Road, Watford garage moving to Garston when that garage was opened in June 1952. A small allocation of these buses was operated by Grays during the period 1954 through to 1956. Interestingly, T794 later moved into the Central Area being operated by Kingston and Norbiton garages from 1956 to 1958 although always retaining its green livery. It was finally withdrawn from service in late 1959 then being exported to Ceylon. (Peter Gulland)

Sun shines on the well stocked travel information building at Sevenoaks bus station as RF653 departs for Chipstead on route 413 complete with the stepped down style of route blinds. There is an air of patience about the queue at Stop 1 who are very tidily attired in an age before jeans and the mini had become fashionable. (R.Wellings)

Although the 2RT2 class was withdrawn from Central Area service at the end of May, seven were repainted into Lincoln green livery and sent to Hertford garage during May to operate route 327 from the 1st June. This was because they were 15cwt. lighter than their post-war counterparts and would not cause the collapse of a somewhat dodgy Metropolitan Water Board bridge which the route crossed at Broxbourne. No destination blind is carried in this view of RT79 and instead a blind from one of the replaced 18STL20s has to suffice for the time being. (A.B.Cross)

Public service does not appear to be the new role for this once 6Q6 Green Line coach. Curtains now adorn the windows along the length of the vehicle while outside illumination has been cleverly added to the front blind box aperture. Newer side light markers have been fixed to the side of the vehicle and one wonders if these are additional to those originally provided within the headlight assemblies. A badge of some description now adorns the front above the radiator grille. The coach was photographed on 30th August at Smedervero, Serbia in the former Yugoslavia. (J.C.Gillham)

Already well laden, RLH59 takes more passengers on board while behind empty looking RT3795 and its driver look on. The RT operates from Sutton garage while Merton houses the RLH, the only Central Area garage south of the Thames ever to operate this small class of lowbridge buses. (J.Gascoine collection)

Putney Bridge garage began receiving RTWs on 1st March for the change over to this type of vehicle for route 14. On 29th March RTW113 makes its way to Kings Cross, St.Pancras passing one of the many Blakey Morris retail wallpaper and paint outlets which sadly have all vanished in the name of progress to be superseded for the most part by the out of town DIY superstore. (A.B.Cross)

RTL199 pauses in Plumstead High Street near Plumstead Station while operating on route 99 which will take the bus as far as Erith, Prince of Wales. This is a remarkably stable route having first plied between Woolwich and Erith on 1st May 1916 although it did suffer a gap in operation in 1919/20. Some attention appears to have been given to the roof joining strips as the glossy finish to them stands out against the duller condition of the roof overall. (A.B.Cross)

GS46 seems to have been ousted from its stand by a fine selection of pre and post-war cars. It works the rather rare peak hour route 451 and displays the destination Hartley Hill instead of the more usual Hartley Court as it waits at Gravesend. Note that the surround of the radiator is now finished in the basic body colour which does nothing to enhance the appearance of this small capacity bus. (R.Wellings)

Elsewhere in this book country bus RFs can be seen on route 342 at the eastern end of this route; Broxbourne and the occasional terminus at Nazeing Gate. Here is route 342 at its western terminus, New Barnet Station, this time with Green Line coach RF85. (G.A.Rixon)

Red liveried RT1473, having been transferred to Staines garage on the 11th July now finds itself on 1st August operating from Windsor garage. This is Bank Holiday Monday and elsewhere in this book you will see a loaned RTL working from Staines garage on the same day. This was all part of the "musical chairs" policy which made these holiday days so fascinating to the contemporary enthusiasts. The unmistakable buildings of Windsor garage together with summer attired prospective passengers waiting in an orderly queue provide the background. To the right of the picture green liveried RT3457, also carrying blinds for route 335, gives intending passengers the choice of whether they prefer a green or red bus to travel in to Watford. With the introduction of the Country Area winter programme the Craven bodied RT would find itself put into store at Stockwell garage together with others of the type pending their further use or eventual disposal. (A.B.Cross)

On loan from Clapham garage red liveried RTL825 operates from Staines garage working a short journey on route 441 to Beaconsfield on Bank Holiday Monday 1st August. Unusually for these sort of loans, Staines garage has fitted a proper set of blinds. It was in February of this year that this vehicle had received its first overhaul which accounts for its pristine condition. The body now carried is number 4178 which was first mounted on RTL778. (A.B.Cross)

Route 52A commenced on 30th November being serviced by eight RTs from Edgware and five RTLs from Willesden garages. The new service was basically a local section of the long lived route 52 which operated as far as Victoria in central London. Running between Colindale trolleybus depot and Borehamwood, Brook Road, the new route included an Express section during Monday to Friday peaks and shopping hours on Saturdays. Willesden's RTL1111 is seen at Colindale with white on blue "EXPRESS" blinds passing an assortment of cars being offered for sale by A.Owen (Hendon) Ltd. who were dealers in many makes of vehicle judging by the names displayed on their fascia. (D.A.Ruddom collection)

RTL68 was transferred into Mortlake garage in March 1955 having spent time at Plumstead since receiving its first overhaul in February 1953. It waits at Richmond Bus Station in August before setting out for Stoke Newington on route 73. (Laurence E.Mallett)

GS45 with a demure notice proclaiming "Please pay as you enter" in the quarter light by the doorway waits in the shadows of Dorking bus station before commencing a journey on duty DS18 on route 449 to Ewhurst. This village, south of Dorking and astride the B2127, once had a small London Transport outstation. Alongside an RT lays over on the long haul route 470. (R.H.G.Simpson)

Fruit pickers were treated to something a little different when they stayed over for a few days at Little Betsoms Farm situated just off the main A233 between Biggin Hill and Westerham. Tucked away among the orchards lurked former ST488 complete with sleeping bunks on the top deck, cooking and eating area on the lower. Other refinements provided in this detached residence were curtains all round, a real front door fitted to the original open platform area, electricity and garden furniture – in fact a real home from home feeling was accomplished. The bus, with LGOC ST2 type body number 12194, was disposed of by London Transport to R.L.Daniels in September 1949 though it is not known how or when it arrived "down on the farm" but these views were taken on 29th July 1955. (Roy Hobbs/A.B.Cross)

In the elegant surroundings of Royal Windsor, Amersham garaged RT3179 arrives after its journey over the Chiltern Hills from Berkhamsted and disgorges most of its passengers before continuing on to the bus station. The Standard Vanguard Mark I car would appear to have been a very popular model at the time judging by the number which have managed to creep into the background of so many views which have appeared in this series of books. (R.F.Mack)

Advertising for Biro ball point pens is much diminished nowadays with their universal acceptance and use but in 1955 they were a relatively new replacement for the nibbed pen and ink variety and mass advertising encouraged you to change over although they were still forbidden in some schools. RTL8 carries the message as it waits at The Mitre at Tooting to run into Clapham garage at the end of its stint on peak hour route 104, the full journey of which worked to Embankment, Horse Guards Avenue. (W.Legg)

A Royal Mail Morris van passes in the background as a group of schoolgirls wait for a 470 bus beside GS45 in use on the Dorking local service, route 449, to Chart Downs. Note the total lack of protection for the schoolgirls in the queue in the so-called bus station, something which would not be tolerated in the safety conscious present. (W.J.Haynes)

T751 has just passed the Chiltern Volunteer public house in Sipson Road, West Drayton on its journey to Hounslow Central Station on 15th July. Route 222 has its origins in the Thames Valley route W20 which was renumbered 501 in 1924 and then 222 in 1934. Although it disappeared for ten years from 1961 to 1971 it has returned to operate between Uxbridge and Hounslow albeit in much changed surroundings. (R.Hobbs/A.B.Cross)

This is a view of Holborn Viaduct rather than a bus picture but it serves to illustrate in a small way the standardisation of the London double deck bus fleet in 1955. The photographer did note at the time that the bus coming down Farringdon Street on route 63 was RT3552. The cars are typical of the period and note too the centre of the road parking which was apparently allowed. A post-war Vauxhall saloon, which has its rear door open, carries the first revised front grille design for this model and a pre-war Ford 10 is parked in front. A post-war Austin A30 can be seen parked right up next to the kerb on the left of the picture while on the far right a pre-war Austin 10 of about 1934/35 vintage is seen. Holborn Viaduct, which was completed in 1869 at a cost of £2.5 million overcame the steep descent into the Fleet Valley previously necessary on the major east-west thoroughfare from the West End to the City. (J.H.Price)

Pictured under trolleybus wiring RM2 on a test run in flat grey primer has stopped at a pedestrian crossing allowing this chance photograph to be taken. Stress testing marks from its first period at the MIRA proving grounds are just discernible centrally under the four normal size top deck windows. At this time the only external difference of this second RM compared to the first was the replacement of the slightly fussy front end treatment of RM1 in favour of a more conventional grille, aided no doubt by the fitment of a radiator in the upright position immediately at the front of the vehicle. The first prototype had a horizontally fitted example with assistance from a large wire mesh enclosed fan because there was no room available with the 9.6 litre engine being fitted. RM2 on the other hand carried the smaller 7.7 litre power plant.

Withdrawn buses and coaches found themselves in use in many guises once discarded by their original operators. This example is totally disguised except for its registration number ELP176, which reveals that the chassis of ex-STL2514 is lurking underneath a Kean built pantechnicon body. Even the tail board is being used to carry someone's prized possessions which cannot be very good for the rear suspension. A small number of STLs were converted in this manner almost certainly due to the low interior floor height available on former bus chassis.

RF26 through to RF288 were the original Green Line batch of coaches within the RF class and were introduced into service between October 1951 and November 1952. These vehicles allowed the 10T10, TF and 6Q6 coaches to be dispersed around the fleet for other duties or withdrawn from service and disposed. Three separate blocks of registration numbers issued by the London office of the licencing authority at the time were used for the RF coaches: LYF377-476, MLL513-612 and MLL763-825. RF282 works as WR72 on route 704 to Tunbridge Wells using the recently introduced style of Green Line route blind in conjunction with the traditional route board. NLE562 parked further along the Windsor bus station roadway is a Country Area bus, RF562, being pressed into Green Line use on route 718 and fitted with route blinds of the type now being phased out. (J.Fozard)

Typical housing, which will have been seen by many tourists to Yugoslavia in its heyday as a holiday destination for the British, completes this picture of a 6Q6. In 1955 this ex-Green Line coach could also be seen, still very recognisable as a London vehicle. It would seem that the side mounted engine has defeated any project to adapt the body to pavement loading as was done with the LT single decker seen elsewhere in this volume. Note the spare wheel which sits in the cab alongside the driver. (National Tramway Museum/N.N.Forbes)

Red liveried RT1486 with Craven body stands in the yard at Staines garage ready for duty on limited stop service 493 which ran on Wednesdays and Saturdays between Englefield Green and St.Peter's Hospital at Botleys Park. After a month garaged at Staines the bus moved on to Windsor for a three month period before moving back into its original sphere of operation in the Central Area. (A.B.Cross)

On 30th June 1954 route 720A was introduced to run between Aldgate and the expanding new town of Harlow. It followed route 720 out of London as far as Potter Street and then made its way to "The Stow" in this new overspill area while the parent route passed through Old Harlow and Sawbridgeworth to reach its destination of Bishops Stortford. RF119 stands at Aldgate with older style front blinds and a side board which appears to be a route 720 example which has been modified for the new route. The coach was transferred from Grays to Epping in June 1954 presumably to cover the extra vehicle requirement for the new route. The poor paint condition of the roof in this 1955 view confirms that it still has to receive its first overhaul later in the year having been in service since January 1952. (Roy Marshall)

Ex-D126 was disposed in May 1953 to the dealer, W.North & Sons who then promptly sold the Daimler CWA6 on to Taylor of Leigh. The bus then passed to another Leigh operator by the name of Davies in whose ownership the vehicle is seen. Just a few months after this photograph was taken the vehicle with its Brush body moved on again to Beeline Roadways of West Hartlepool finally finishing its career with the Executors of Samuel Ledgard who by then were operating a number of ex-London Daimlers which had been bought with the proceeds from the sale of a large number of unroadworthy vehicles. (Real Photographs)

On 12th October route 91 was diverted away from its long standing terminus at the Queen's Head, Cranford to operate through to London Airport Central. Road/rail through tickets were available on this route via Hounslow West station to London Airport. Standing at the Wandsworth Bridge terminus, RTL1390 from Riverside garage looks smartly turned out although the painted wheel trims rather spoil the effect. (W.Legg)

The original RF523 operates the 440 route between Salfords and Redhill and passes the Redhill Station building as it emerges from the railway bridges which cross the A25 at this point. At Salfords, south of Redhill, the route terminated at the Monotype Works in Honeycrock Lane. The gleaming radiator of a Standard 12/14 model car catches the sun's rays. (Surfleet Transport Photographs)

RT4225 stands at Leytonstone on 12th March with the leafless extremities of Wanstead Flats in the background before running to Debden on route 20A. The bus had been transferred into Loughton garage days earlier from Holloway and was one of the vehicles which initiated RT operation from this north-east outpost of the Central Area and sealed the fate of the last post-war STDs. (J.Gascoine collection)

At the same Vauxhall location in which an RT on Route 69 appears earlier in the book, nicely turned out RT203 works the long established Route 36. Note that it is carrying a body of the type originally fitted when it entered service in October 1947, verified by the small offside route number plate. Although it has lost its cream surround to the upper deck windows it now carries a full set of route blinds denied to it in its early years. (R.Wellings)

What was once C41 is now in use with James Miller and Partners (contractors) of Wakefield, Yorkshire who had acquired it sometime during 1955 from W.North, the dealers of Leeds to whom LTE had initially sold the vehicle. First entering service from Guildford garage in June 1935 it continued in service from a number of different Country Area garages until replaced by a new GS class vehicle while operating from Tring in February 1954. (R.F.Mack)

With the seemingly eternal chestnut trees now in full bloom at Hampton Court on 4th June, red liveried RT1498 makes its way to Kingston, then the eastern terminus of route 131 from Walton-on-Thames. The double deck version of pre-war route 214, the route was to figure seven years later in the trolleybus replacement programme and forty years on in 1995 Kingston would be the western terminus of the route from Wimbledon. (J.C.Gillham)

In 1955 the South Kensington – Festival Gardens summer service was numbered 45A and RTL965 stands at the South Kensington terminus. A London Transport conference appears to be in progress, perhaps discussing the necessity of the operation judging by the deserted surroundings. The dolly stop placed in the middle of the road is probably intended to show the more normal stand for these buses which was in the centre of the carriageway. (R.Wellings)

This fine line-up of some of the ex-STLs operated by Rush & Tompkins (contractors) of Sidcup, Kent needs some help in identification. From left to right they are: STL1662, a 4/9STL11; STL1802, a 4/9STL14; STL1351, a 3/9STL11; STL660, a 9STL11 with STL2515, a 4/9STL12 completing the row. Here in 1955 they are rather nicely presented with Rush & Tompkins paper stickers in the via box apertures although they were not destined to last for long and by October 1958 none would be left in service. (P.J.Marshall)

Some of the paraphernalia associated with a private operator surrounds what is left of ST140 in the Strood yard of J.W.H.Watson who operated as Wilberjim Coaches. The bus had originally entered service as a 50 seat lowbridge vehicle in May 1930 being operated by the National Omnibus and Transport Co.Ltd. on behalf of the LGOC. When delivered it was painted red, a colour continued by the subsequent London General Country Services Ltd. It was repainted into the Country Area green livery soon after the formation of the Board. In August 1941 it was again repainted red for Central Area service but in November 1944 reverted to its former Country Area colours being withdrawn from service in October 1952. Disposed of to W.North of Leeds in March 1953 it was then acquired by Watson in the following month. This photograph was taken on 24th June 1955 and shows the bus cut down and converted as a general purpose lorry having practically reached the end of its long life. (R.Hobbs/A.B.Cross)

Two ex-London Guys now in Western SMT colours stand parked in the Carlisle garage entrance waiting further use soon after a recent downpour as the tyre marks confirm. On the left of the photograph ex-G157 is still carrying its original NCME body with fleet number DY1022. Ex-G178 on the right has been rebodied in 1954 with a secondhand Croft built 53 seat lowbridge body and now carries fleet number DY1051. (A.B.Cross)

Ex-T314 finished its days in use as a caravan at Erith Railway Farm depot and now looks in a very sorry state and likely to be enveloped by the encroaching heaps of gravel. First entering service with Tillings in October 1932 it was taken over by the LPTB in October 1933 and gave many years of service chiefly in the Kingston area until it was disposed of to R.L.Daniels in August 1949. It had been first noted at Erith in November 1953, its history between disposal and this sighting remains a mystery.

RTL618 operating from West Green garage enters Trafalgar Square on route 29A heading for Victoria. This route was introduced on a Monday to Saturday basis on 12th October by extending half of the Victoria – Southgate journeys on route 29 to Oakwood Station via Chase Road and renumbering them 29A. Because of the longer journey time West Green gained an extra RTL to keep a compatible frequency. The through service from Victoria to Oakwood only lasted for a year and in October 1956 the Oakwood service was "suburbanised" being removed south of Turnpike Lane Station. (W.J.Haynes)

Former B10 was acquired by the Lincolnshire Road Car Company Ltd. in January 1953 and allocated fleet number 979. The bus had been withdrawn by LTE in September 1951 after only five and a half years service within the capital and as with other wartime deliveries withdrawn around the same period must have represented a good buy for their new owners with their relatively low mileage. In 1953 the entire fleet owned by Lincolnshire Road Car was renumbered and this Bristol K6A with modified Duple 56 seat body became fleet number 2106. (N.Anscombe collection)

A busy scene in Richmond town centre while RT1755 disgorges some of its passengers to swell even further the congestion on the narrow pavement. This RT is garaged at Holloway having previously been at Croydon and Forest Gate since receiving its first overhaul during the previous year. (J.Gascoine collection)

GS78 is seen in Slough employed on route 442 while making its way to Farnham Royal in the early part of the year. It still carries the first type of "Please Pay As You Enter" notice in the top of the nearside front window. It was during this period that the square shaped notice fixed to the nearside triangular window beside the entrance appeared. Fifteen higher numbered vehicles of this class spent their first few months in store at Garston and Reigate garages before entering service at different times during 1954 and this particular vehicle was one of them. (C.Carter)

RTL607 stands at Abbey Wood early in the year prior to the conversion of this South East London garage from Leyland to AEC vehicles. Previously a tram depot, bus operation had commenced on 6th July 1952 with RTLs, the day after the last tramway operation in London. The 177 route was the replacement for Tram Services 36 and 38 and was another route provided with experimental three line via point blinds. (Peter Gulland)

RFW4 with a full load on a London Airport Tour passes the Chiswick bus overhaul works. Trolleybus wiring is in place for routes which would be among the last survivors seven years hence on 8th May 1962 after which diesel would reign supreme. (R.H.G.Simpson)

Not too many buses have passed the white marble memorial to Queen Victoria in front of Buckingham Palace at the end of the Mall but this RT 1715 is privileged to do so while working route 19. For some reason, probably road works in Piccadilly, buses were diverted during August along roads which took them through these prestigious surroundings. This view on Saturday 20th August shows a remarkable lack of tourists in the area. (J.H.Price)

Ex-STD140 appears to have been put straight into service in Yugoslavia upon delivery as it still carries its British registration, empty blind boxes and a sticker in the front bulkhead window with route details which read "Split – Trogdir". Eventually a local registration and a proper set of route blinds would be necessary but just for now that can wait.

(N.N.Forbes/National Tramway Museum)

Leaving Luton with a good load of shoppers for its journey via the "lower road" to Wheathampstead and St.Albans, RF549 will continue beyond the town centre at St.Albans to Hill End, probably with a new load of shoppers. This bus dates from May 1953 and in this view still resides at its initially allocated garage of St.Albans who had previously operated 4Q4 type vehicles among others on this route. (R.Wellings)

Pictured at the old Southmill Road terminus at Bishops Stortford, STL2685 operates on route 350A on 21st May just over a week before being withdrawn from service along with the other 18STL20s operated by Hertford garage. On 5th October the route would be extended from this terminus in Bishops Stortford to the newly developed Havers Lane Estate. No additional buses were needed for this since a tightening up of the schedule meant that the average journey time for the extended route was six minutes less. (J.C.Gillham)

Hardly recognisable now, ex-D15 waits to be panelled at the Harkness Coachbuilding works premises in Belfast. The bus had been disposed of to W.North in September 1953 arriving at its new owners, Belfast Corporation, later in the year. Entering service with its original Duple body, it was not until the period 1955/56 that all the fifty Daimlers acquired were rebodied. (W.Montgomery)

The only additional operating centre for buses and coaches brought into use during the year was the temporary premises at Fishers Green Road, Stevenage. The building and adjoining small plot of land containing the ancillary equipment had previously been used by British Road Services and was desperately needed to reduce dead mileage and pressure on Hitchin garage due to the increasingly expanding services in the New Town. Although termed temporary it was to be used continuously until a new garage was opened nearer the new town centre in 1959. RF618 is parked nose first within the garage while an RT has been reversed into the small parking area.
(London Transport Museum 1274/2)

Rennell Street, Lewisham on 12th February provides the resting place for RT920 and RT1273 while engaged on route 89 and soon to depart for Welling, Guy Earl of Warwick. Route 89's frequency had been reduced on 5th January when new route 89A replaced route 256 between Woolwich and Shooters Hill and continued alongside 89 to Lewisham. (A.B.Cross)

Nearing its first overhaul with fading paintwork and damaged body, RF136 operates as HN70 with a side route board which has seen better days. At least it sports a new style set of blinds which display its intent to return home on route 716 to Hitchin from Chertsey. This was the coach which in 1965/66 would be used as the prototype for the modernisation of these vehicles. (Lens of Sutton)

The first northern country area route to experience one-man operation using the larger RF class vehicles was the 316 from Chesham to Hemel Hempstead, which was jointly operated with J.G.Dell's Rover Bus Services. RF647, one of the original trio of OMO vehicles in the class, carries its barely visible "Pay As You Enter" sticker at the top of the nearside front window as it stands in Chesham Broadway with blinds still to be changed for its return journey to Hemel Hempstead. (R.Lunn)

Excursion No.20 from Maryland Station to Whipsnade only operated on Bank Holidays in 1955. RTL1417, garaged at Clay Hall, has on this occasion made the trip to this beautiful part of the Bedfordshire countryside and has been left on the grass parking area of the Zoo in company with other London Transport vehicles and some fine looking cars. (D.A.Jones)

As might be expected the 29th January was a cold and dull day. In the gloom RT116 pauses at its first stop on its way to Kingston on route 85 on the north side of Putney Bridge. Nobody in the queue seems very interested so they are probably awaiting one of the six other routes which this stop serves. (G.Mead)

Green liveried RLH12 operated all its London Transport life from Addlestone garage and was even stored there from its withdrawal in June 1965 until sold in February 1966. In happier times it is seen here at the Onslow Street Bus Station in Guildford about to pull away on duty WY17 on route 463 over to Walton on 9th October. (J.C.Gillham)

RT840 stands in front of the rebuilt Hounslow garage which had been opened the previous year. The history of the site as a garage goes back to 1913 when the LGOC opened the original building on the track of a former short branch line of the District Railway which terminated at Hounslow Town Station on the north side of London Road. The arches of the viaduct carrying this line were incorporated into the old garage but all has been swept away by 1955 with the new bus station and garage. Note that just three lines of intermediate points were all that was considered necessary to cover the 117 route from Hounslow to Egham Station and the neat simplicity of the display suits the roof box body. (C.Carter)

New Cross garage last operated the 2RT2 type on 16th May. Previous to this on 22nd April, RT15 works on route 186 which originally replaced the eastern section of tram route 72 and the western section of bus route 94 in July 1952. Here the bus is seen at the leafless Crystal Palace stand in company with RT419. This 3RT with body number 1668 was one of the earliest to be disposed of after the Craven bodied examples had been dealt with.

RF574 in the parking area at Broxbourne Station, presumably having the authorisation the British Railways sign requires, waits for its return journey to New Barnet via Hertford on route 342. A few passengers have availed themselves of the open door policy and taken their seats in readiness to have their fares collected by the conductor when the crew returns. (J.H.Aston)

Q type buses operated route 241 until two batches of new RFs were delivered to Sidcup garage in the final month of 1952 and the first of 1953. RF479 waits at Welling with an old style blind, which doubtless has seen service in a Q, before departing for the southern terminus of the route at Sidcup garage in Foots Cray. (D.A.Ruddom collection)

Chelverton Road, Putney garage started to receive post-war RT class buses on 15th February and since the garage was converted to Leyland operation in the spring, their appearance at AF was very short lived. RT4071 was received in March remaining only a few weeks before moving on to Abbey Wood garage and here on 30th March it is in use on route 28 as it waits at the Wandsworth High Street stand in Wandsworth Plain. (A.B.Cross)

On a snowy 4th January a varied line up of vehicles await their inevitable fate in this bleak scene at Chiswick Works. From right to left are CR4, T646, later noted operating in the Canary Islands, STL2501, which operated for Comfort Coaches of Dunfermline in later years, STL1101, an unidentifiable C and STL1940 with beyond a further 10T10 and an STL. Maybe STL2501 did go to Comfort Coaches but for the moment it is cold comfort indeed! (J.C.Gillham)

Mann Egerton bodied TD58, having only recently been transferred into Norbiton garage from its previous home at Hornchurch, disgorges its passengers in Cromwell Road, Kingston before it turns right into the bus garage. The date is 29th January, which accounts for the gloomy conditions which prevail. (A.B.Cross)

Arriving at the Wembley Stadium complex with a heavy load of passengers RFW7 shows that its trafficator arm is still in good working order – or is it stuck out permanently? The 3RF3 coded long distance and private hire coaches seated 39 in their ECW built bodies which were mounted on AEC Regal Mark IV 9821E chassis. (R.H.G.Simpson)

With the Epsom Race Course grandstand in the background and an Austin taxi to the left of the picture, which partially hides a Mark VII Jaguar, RT1449 makes its way back to Epsom Station. Typical of the race meetings of the era, a steady stream of buses kept plying their way between the course and Epsom or Morden Underground Station, unlike today's involvement of roughly a dozen or so vehicles. (G.A.Rixon)

Recently overhauled and nicely turned out RT1953 operates from Thornton Heath garage on route 109 to Purley High Street. It would continue to be allocated to TH until September 1958. Nearly forty years on and the two advertiser's products can still be purchased to warm one's inner man, according to your fancy. (Roy Marshall)

This rear view of RFW8 clearly shows the reflectors which have been added to the rear luggage boot doors. The rear light markers at roof level and those fitted to the extreme corner panelling lower down were incorporated in the ECW body when new. The London Transport bullseye transfer mounted in the centre of the rear window now looks a little faded and tatty and with the originally polished rear wheel trim and extreme bottom beading now painted over, the touring coach is sadly no longer in its pristine condition of a few years ago. (R.H.Simpson)

An unidentified STL class vehicle shows the lengths the operator has gone to in making the bus suitable for operation in a country where the rule of the road is on the right. The original open rear platform has been panelled and glazed and a sliding door added to the rear of the vehicle which allows access from behind to the original platform. It almost appears as if the potential passengers are bartering a price for the journey from this suburban terminus of route 4 to the centre of Skopje in Macedonia, being part of Yugoslavia on 7th September. The nearside blind box has been neatly adapted for an advertisement. (J.C.Gillham)

RT4196 was transferred into Grays in August after its first overhaul, having previously been garaged at Staines since new in July 1951. Here it stands at the Tilbury Ferry terminus of route 370 while the driver watches the activity on the river. (Frank Church)

Ex-Q88 once saw service as a Green Line coach as shown by the radiator grille for the cooling system which had been moved to this new position. The remains of the brackets above the side windows for route boards can also be detected. Having last operated as a Country Area bus from Watford, Leavesden Road garage it was withdrawn from service in February 1952 and disposed to F.Cowley before being purchased by F.W.Shanks Ltd. (contractors) of Hunstanton, Norfolk. In the background is one of the last real Riley cars, a 1½ or 2½ litre model.
(N.Anscombe collection)

Six of the Country Area batch of thirty four 17STLs delivered in 1941 and 1942 were chosen to be converted into service vehicles at the end of their passenger carrying lives. FXT384, now known as 1018J a shelter carrier, was once STL2661 plying for passengers from Godstone, High Wycombe, Luton and Watford High Street garages, all of which are now but a memory. The vehicle is photographed at Uxbridge on 2nd September having been in use in its new capacity for just a year. (A.G.Newman)

This further view of RTL1117 in the unfamiliar surroundings of the Velperplien in Arnham quite clearly demonstrates the continental approach to advertising. Enthusiastic townspeople board the bus for a half hour flip round the town for 25 cents in aid of the Eutopia festival then taking place. The crew drawn from Reigate thoroughly enjoyed themselves during their visit, helped in no small measure by the warmth shown to them which the Dutch people are renowned for. (N.Rothon)

New building work progresses at the Uxbridge Bus Station behind the Underground Station while T764 operating on route 224 to Harmondsworth awaits for its departure time to arrive on 2nd September. Several passengers have availed themselves of the seating provided within the Weymann bodied AEC Regal of 1946 manufacture. For the technically minded the batch of fifty buses comprising the 14T12 sub-class were powered by 7.7 litre engines through a crash gearbox to the rear wheel drive and were also fitted with triple-servo braking. (A.G.Newman)

Another Bank Holiday Monday shot in Oxted shows GS10 on its way from Holland to Edenbridge on route 465. In 1953 the GS class had replaced the Leyland C class which had previously worked Chelsham's routes which necessitated smaller buses. In 1977 Ray Stenning wrote an article in the London Bus Magazine about these routes and referred to the GS as "The Puppy Bus", a very apt name for this pleasant diminutive vehicle. (J.H.Aston)

A further picture of the short lived route 852 in its original form before the Ewhurst to Horsham section was replaced by A.T.Brady's Brown Motor Services on 18th May. GS83 is pictured at Ewhurst on 19th April and the picture emphasises the size and rake of the steering wheel on the GS class. (A.G.Newman)

Route 388A was only operated from 15th December 1954 through to 20th March 1956 to provide a local service for the inhabitants of Sele Farm Estate. During the summer at Hertford Bus Station GS73 operates the route to Sele Farm Estate while alongside GS18 works the main route through to Welwyn, Prospect Place. Both buses were operated by Hertford garage at the time, GS73 having spent a while stored at Garston when new. Note the handles fitted either side at the bottom of the windscreen. Although a small area on the top of the front wings of these vehicles was covered with flooring metal strips to provide a foothold for anyone needing to reach the front route blind box, it was soon realised that a grab handle would be useful and so eventually those as fitted by the cab doors of RTs were fitted to all of the class in this way for this purpose. (John Lines collection)

The post-war batch of twenty AEC Regents with Weymann 56 seat highbridge bodywork numbered STL2682 to 2701 were all withdrawn and disposed of to W.North of Leeds in July or August of the year under review. They all quickly found new homes and what was the first of the batch, STL2682, is seen in Widnes town centre embellished with the Corporation's coat of arms and carrying fleet number 22. Little change has been made to the vehicle though trafficators have been added and the route blind box aperture has been altered to take two blinds with the addition of black tape. The bus is actually en-route to Farnworth although from this angle the F is not visible. (J.G.E.Nye)

APPENDIX I

London Transport Central and Country Area Bus Garages

A	Sutton	K	Kingston
AB	Twickenham	L	Loughton
AC	Willesden	LH*	Leatherhead
AD	Palmers Green	LS*	Luton
AE	Hendon	M	Mortlake
AF	Chelverton Road, Putney	MA*	Amersham
AK	Streatham	MH	Muswell Hill
AL	Merton	N	Norwood
AM	Plumstead	NB	Norbiton
AP	Seven Kings	NF*	Northfleet
AR	Tottenham	NS	North Street, Romford
AV	Hounslow	NX	New Cross
AW	Abbey Wood	ON	Alperton
B	Battersea	P	Old Kent Road
BK	Barking	PB	Potters Bar
BN	Brixton	PM	Peckham
C	Athol Street, Poplar	Q	Camberwell
CA	Clapham	R	Riverside
CF	Chalk Farm	RD	Hornchurch
CL	Clay Hall	RE*	London Road, Romford
CM*	Chelsham	RG*	Reigate
CS	Chiswick (non-operational)	RL	Rye Lane
CY*	Crawley	S	Shepherds Bush
D	Dalston	SA*	St Albans
DG*	Dunton Green	SJ*	Swanley Junction
DS*	Dorking	SP	Sidcup
DT*	Dartford	ST*	Staines
E	Enfield	SW	Stockwell
ED	Elmers End	T	Leyton
EG*	East Grinstead	TB	Bromley
EP*	Epping	TC	Croydon
EW	Edgware	TG*	Tring
F	Putney Bridge	TH	Thornton Heath
G	Forest Gate	TL	Catford
GD*	Godstone	TW*	Tunbridge Wells
GF*	Guildford	U	Upton Park
GM	Gillingham Street, Victoria	UX	Uxbridge
GR*	Garston	V	Turnham Green
GY*	Grays	W	Cricklewood
H	Hackney	WA*	Watford, High Street
HD	Harrow Weald	WD	Wandsworth
HE*	High Wycombe	WG	West Green
HF*	Hatfield	WL	Walworth
HG*	Hertford	WR*	Windsor
HH*	Two Waters, Hemel Hempstead	WY*	Addlestone
HN*	Hitchin	X	Middle Row
HW	Southall	–	Aldenham (non-operational)
J	Holloway	* indicates a Country Area garage.	

The above list is of all operational garages plus the two main non-operational sites for bus maintenance available on 1st January 1955.

During the year only one additional garage was added to the list quoted above. A part brick, part corrugated iron structure previously owned by British Road Services situated in Fishers Green Road, Stevenage was brought into use on 5th October using garage code SV. The initial allocation was six RTs and two RFs and with its introduction pressure on Hitchin was reduced with "dead" mileage incurred by the buses used on Stevenage town services greatly diminished.

APPENDIX II

Thanks to correspondence from interested enthusiasts this Appendix is provided to enhance information in previously published books in this series.

1939/45 BOOK

Page16	The registration number in the caption should read V0561<u>2</u>.
Page 20	It is ST602 which is also included in the upper picture.
Page 26	The busy bus station in the upper picture is Gloucester Green at Oxford.
Page 51	The lower picture depicts an overnight dispersal point for a south-east London garage, possibly Sidcup, hence the 5Q5 which is just visible.
Page 58	In the upper picture UC2294 became staff canteen 40H and not 33H as stated.
Page 59	The upper photograph shows buses in the Bayswater Road looking westward towards Lancaster Gate. The <u>east</u>bound LT1293 on route 23 has been unable to enter Oxford Street and has been forced to divert westwards along Bayswater Road to seek some means of returning to east London. The two Bluebird LTs on route 17 are probably aiming to turn back at Marble Arch. At this juncture in time the Royal Park's chairs have been set in this manner to mark the park boundary following the removal of the railings.
	The TFs in the lower picture are parked at the western end of The Embankment in Putney alongside Leaders Gardens, the railings of which appear to have escaped the attention of the war effort as they are still in situ to this day.
Page 65	The RT (FXT213) in Shaftesbury Avenue is RT38 not RT28.
Page 75	Route 254 did not disappear until the start of September 1940 as correctly stated on page 80.
Page 86	B8 is seen at Ealing Broadway. The clock outside Poole's the jewellers is known to have still been there in November 1968!
Page 87	G39 is standing in Fore Street at the original London bound stop at the Angel, Edmonton just north of Angel Road.
Page 127	The cream surrounds referred to in the caption should of course be broken white.
Page 154	It has been pointed out that according to Ken Blacker's book "The STLs" STL1920, which features in the lower picture, received its blast damage in September 1943. The body, number 17240 of the STL14 variety, was eventually repaired and mounted on the chassis of STL1770. My correspondent suggests that the most likely place for the incident to have occurred was on Angel Road at the Edmonton factory colony.
Page 155	RV1143 in the lower picture is of course a Tilling-Stevens and not a Leyland TD1.
Page 158	WT* Watford, Leavesden Road has been inadvertently omitted from the list of garages.
Page 160	In the correction to page 87 of the 1953 book it is STL2147 which is seen in Dartford and not as stated STL2543 whose body is mentioned in the original caption to the photograph.

1949 BOOK

Page 78	The ST body, number 13922, mounted on the RT test rig was that latterly mounted on the chassis of ex-Tilling ST977.

1950 BOOK

Page 52   The upper photograph shows STL1310 approaching "The Pickhurst" public house stop.

Page 108   RLH16 in the lower photograph is pulling away from the stop at Godstone Green.

1953 BOOK

Page 78   The RTL included in the lower picture is RTL1410 (MXX217) not RTL410.

Page 160   It is STL287 confirmed by its registration number AUC541 and not STL278 which is the subject of this photograph.

1954 BOOK

Page 38   The ST body, number 13922, mounted on the RT test rig was that latterly mounted on the chassis of ex-Tilling ST977.

Page 52   The upper picture depicts RT1274 and not RT1283.

Page 117   Left and below the "Typhoo" RT is a power assisted cycle fitted with a "Cyclemaster" rear wheel which was a popular means of transport for a number of years around this era. Did you spot it?

A much loved Austin Seven keeps RT3726 company while they stand outside the White Hart public house in the old town of Crawley in this lovely view of a carefree and relaxed era now lost forever. The Crawley garaged bus is operating a section of route 426 between Ifield and Two Bridges providing an embryonic New Town service. (R.Wellings)